30 minute Asian meals made simple

Exclusive to Howdens Joinery Co.

Seiko Hatfield

30 minute Asian meals made simple

Although we all have busy lives these days, we still want to make interesting, tasty meals – and to try exciting new dishes. This book helps you do that, quickly and easily, with authentic recipes from six Asian countries: China, Japan, Korea, Malaysia, Thailand and Vietnam. Each has its own distinctive style of cooking, and I want to show you simple ways to recreate this wonderful variety of flavours at home.

Whether you're an experienced cook or just learning, these recipes will show you how to produce authentic Asian meals in 30 minutes or less. So even if you're in a hurry to make a midweek family supper, you'll find plenty of ideas to help you be more adventurous in the kitchen. And if you're entertaining, you'll see how you can impress your guests while saving precious time.

I've cooked all these recipes using Lamona appliances, so I know you can look forward to fantastic results. With reliable equipment in a well-designed kitchen from Howdens Joinery, you'll really enjoy exploring the diversity of Asian cooking.

I hope this cookbook inspires you to discover more about the food of these six fascinating countries.

Seiko Hatfield

Food Stylist and Writer

The Asian Kitchen

Across Asia, cooking good food is a great source of pride which is reflected in the design of this kitchen. Imaginative open storage spaces have been created to show off beautifully presented dishes and display items effortlessly, while the L-shaped bench brings guests and family members closer to the cooking experience.

Hidden storage solutions keep the overall look tidy, sleek and simple. Dark colours set the tone, with paler, neutral highlights, natural finishes and soft red accents, symbolising the happiness, joy and celebration of Asian cooking.

Our Asian Connection

At Howdens, we recognise the importance of selecting the right business partners that carry similar values to our own. Creating productive, lasting relationships with carefully selected businesses is critical to our long-term success.

Building relationships with local communities is also an essential part of Howdens' business philosophy. Howdens was set up to be 'worthwhile for all concerned', with staff, customers and suppliers contributing to make this a daily reality within the communities they live in. To read stories about how our staff are supporting their local communities, visit www.howdens.com/about-us/a-truly-local-business.

Howdens and JELD-WEN have been working together since 2008, and have formed a strong partnership. Corinthian Doors, based near Kuala Lumpar, Malaysia, is part of the JELD-WEN group of companies, and supplies some of our finest joinery products, including hardwood internal and external doors, and primed stile and rail doors.

Aligned to Howdens' own values, JELD-WEN is an active supporter of the local community, whose members are the backbone of their workforce.

JELD-WEN recognised that the local village school was in desperate need of state of the art technology, enabling students to keep up to date with the latest education developments. JELD-WEN donated 10 new computers, making a huge difference to the children educated in this village school.

Additionally, JELD-WEN recently embarked on a joint program with WISDEC (Wood Industry Skills Development Centre) and MTIB (Malaysian Timber Industry Board) to sponsor industrial trainees and provide work placements for them within their organisation, leading to permanent employment once they successfully completed their apprenticeships.

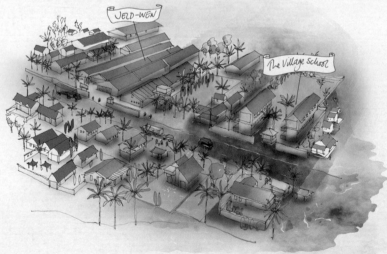

JELD·WEN®

The John Hedgecock
Memorial Award
Winner
2011

(v) = vegetarian

CHINESE

Chinese cooking is incredibly varied, ranging from rich, highly spiced Szechuan dishes to the more delicate flavours of mountainous regions such as Anhui. I hope this collection of recipes will encourage you to try something new at home which is deliciously different from what you will usually find in Cantonese restaurants in the UK.

Serves 4
(about 12 dumplings)
20 mins preparation
8 mins cooking

Prawn Siu Mai

Prawn Dumplings

Ingredients

150g tiger prawns, shelled and
veins removed
50g fresh bamboo shoots
1 spring onion, finely chopped
¼ teaspoon chopped chives
1 teaspoon sesame oil
1 tablespoon egg white
1 tablespoon cornflour
1 teaspoon grated ginger
¼ teaspoon salt
A few pinches of white pepper
½ teaspoon soy sauce
1 tablespoon strong vegetable or
chicken stock
12 cooked green peas
12 squares of pastry, 7 x 7cm
made with 2 sheets of filo pastry

Equipment

Baking parchment
Steamer

I tried dumplings like this in a busy dim sum café in Hong Kong. Hot and steaming, they were extremely popular, simply because they're so tasty and moreish. My version – filled with prawns, chives and bamboo shoots – is easy to make at home, and just as good as the ones in the café!

1. Pat dry the tiger prawns and bamboo shoots with kitchen paper.

2. Finely chop the prawns with a large knife and put them in a large bowl.

3. Finely chop the bamboo shoots and put them in the same bowl.

4. Add the spring onions, chives, sesame oil, egg white, cornflour, ginger, salt, pepper, soy sauce and stock. Mix well with chopsticks, or use your hands.

5. Place a steamer over a pan of simmering water.

6. Put about 2 teaspoons of the prawn mixture in the centre of each pastry square, and bring the sides up lightly to make frilly drapes. Decorate each with a green pea on top.

7. Place the dumplings on a tray as you make them. When they're all ready, line the steamer with baking parchment and put the dumplings in. Put the lid on and steam for 7-8 minutes. Leave to rest for few minutes before serving.

Chef's note... Traditionally we use wonton pastry for making sui mai. This is available from chinese supermarkets but I have found filo pastry is a quick alternative to use.

If you want to make your own pastry, mix 100g of 00 pasta flour with 75-80ml of water, in a bowl. When you've made a ball, knead it for 1 minute, and then wrap it in cling film. Keep it in the fridge for at least 10 minutes, then roll it out through a pasta machine. Make it as thin as possible and cut into 7 x 7cm squares. You can freeze these to use later – if so, dust them well with flour between the layers.

Stir-Fried Gai Lan

Stir-Fried Broccoli

Broccoli stir-fried with garlic and ginger bursts with fresh flavours, and is extremely wholesome. My mother always added extra vegetable dishes to our dinner table, and I remember looking forward to this, even as a small child. Try it as a side dish with any Chinese main course.

Ingredients

1 litre water
1 teaspoon salt
300g tenderstem broccoli or Chinese broccoli (Gai Lan)
1 tablespoon vegetable oil
½ red chilli, finely sliced
2 garlic cloves, peeled and finely chopped
8 slices ginger, cut into very thin strips
1 teaspoon cornflour
3 tablespoons water
1 tablespoon light soy sauce
2 teaspoons sesame oil
Salt and pepper to season
Sesame seeds to sprinkle on top (optional)

Equipment
Large wok

1. Boil the water in a large pan and add the salt. Add the broccoli to the pan and cook for 3-4 minutes, until it's tender but still has some bite. Drain and put to one side to cool a little.

2. Heat the vegetable oil in a large wok, over a high heat. Add the chilli and fry for 30 seconds, then add the garlic and ginger.

3. Place the broccoli in the wok and fry for 3 minutes, until it's lightly coated with vegetable oil and slightly charred.

4. Combine the cornflour, 3 tablespoons of water and soy sauce in a small bowl, and then pour this over the broccoli. Keep stirring until the cornflour has thickened.

5. Add the sesame oil, and season with salt and pepper. Arrange the broccoli on a large sharing plate, and sprinkle with toasted sesame seeds.

Chef's note... I like my broccoli to have a bit of bite, but if you prefer it softer, cook it for about 5-6 minutes at the first stage.

Crab and Egg Fried Rice

Ingredients

3 medium eggs
A few pinches of salt and pepper
1 tablespoon water
1½ tablespoons groundnut or vegetable oil
2 garlic cloves, finely chopped
1 small onion, finely chopped
500g warm cooked rice (see page 106)
1½ teaspoons sesame oil
240g white crab meat (fresh or tinned)
2 teaspoons light soy sauce
A few pinches of white pepper
2 spring onions, finely chopped
1 small bunch coriander, chopped, plus some more to garnish (optional)
1 teaspoon toasted sesame seeds
1 lime (one half for juice, the other half cut into wedges)

Equipment

Non-stick wok

Crab with egg is a classic combination in Far Eastern cooking, and I like to use it in simple dishes like this delicious fried rice. You can also turn this into a vegetarian recipe very easily – instead of the crab, use other ingredients, such as sweetcorn, soya mince or mushrooms.

1. Crack the eggs into a bowl and add a few pinches of salt and pepper. Add the water to loosen the mixture slightly and mix well.

2. Add half a tablespoon of oil to a non-stick wok over a high heat. When the oil is hot, pour in the egg mixture. Stir occasionally, until the egg has set, and then transfer it to a bowl and keep to one side.

3. Pour the remaining oil into the wok and add the garlic. Fry for a minute, then add the onion. Cook on a medium heat for 1-2 minutes, until the onion turns translucent.

4. Add the cooked rice, making sure the grains aren't lumpy. If you need to loosen the grains, add a few tablespoons of water. If it starts sticking to the wok, you may need to add a little more oil.

5. Now add the sesame oil and crab meat. Fry for a minute, and then add the soy sauce, pepper, spring onions, coriander and sesame seeds.

6. Put the egg back in the pan, stir and fry for a minute.

7. Finally add the juice of half the lime. Stir lightly, and transfer to a large bowl or plate for sharing. Top with extra coriander and lime wedges, and serve.

Sichuan Mapo Tofu

Pork Mince and Silky Tofu in Spicy Sichuan Sauce

Serves 4
10 mins preparation
20 mins cooking

Ingredients

1 litre water
600g silken tofu (2 packs),
cut into 1½cm cubes
1 tablespoon vegetable oil
1 tablespoon sesame oil
3 garlic cloves, finely chopped
2 tablespoons grated ginger
200g minced pork
2 tablespoons Chinese rice wine
(Shaoxing) or sake
2 tablespoons black bean sauce
2 tablespoons chilli bean sauce
300ml chicken stock
2 tablespoons cornflour,
mixed with 40ml water
1 tablespoon light soy sauce
½ teaspoon toasted and ground
Sichuan pepper
1 tablespoon finely chopped
spring onion
Chilli oil, if you want to add more
spicy heat

Equipment

Large frying pan or skillet
Large wok

Mapo Tofu is originally from the Sichuan Province, and is wonderfully spicy and hot. I love cooking my version too – it's milder and lighter, and the combination of silky tofu, pork, chilli and bean sauce works perfectly.

1. In a large frying pan or skillet, bring 1 litre of water to a simmer and add the tofu to poach for a few minutes. Turn off the heat and leave the tofu to keep warm until later.

2. In a large wok, add both oils and fry the garlic and ginger for 1 minute. Add the minced pork, and fry for about 5 minutes or until cooked through over a medium to high heat. Add the Chinese rice wine or sake and continue frying for about a minute, until most of the liquid has evaporated.

3. Meanwhile, carefully transfer the tofu pieces from the simmering water to a colander, and leave to drain for 1 minute.

4. Add the black bean sauce and chilli bean sauce to the wok, and stir well. Pour in the chicken stock and add the tofu pieces. Add the cornflour mix and soy sauce, and stir gently with a wooden spoon until the sauce has thickened slightly.

5. Warm a large bowl and pour in the Mapo Tofu. Sprinkle with the Sichuan pepper and chopped spring onion.

6. Serve with a bowl of rice – and add some chilli oil if you like extra heat.

Chef's note... This is quite a spicy dish. If you prefer a milder flavour, use less chilli bean sauce.

If you want to make a vegetarian version, use soya mince instead of pork and vegetable stock instead of chicken stock.

Bang Bang Ji

Chicken Salad with Sesame and Peanut Dressing

Ingredients

1.2 litres water
4 chicken thighs, boned,
but with the skin on
4 chicken thigh bones (optional)
2 spring onions
4 slices ginger
1 teaspoon black peppercorns
1 teaspoon salt

For the dressing

1½ tablespoons sugar
1 tablespoon rice wine vinegar
3 tablespoons light soy sauce
½ tablespoon sesame oil
½ tablespoon chilli oil
½ teaspoon black bean sauce
2 tablespoons light or dark tahini
(sesame paste)

For the rest of the dish

130g beansprouts
150g lettuce leaves, shredded
2 large tomatoes,
cut into 5mm slices
¼ cucumber, thinly sliced
1-2 tablespoons toasted peanuts,
chopped
2 spring onions,
finely sliced (optional)

When you want something easy, Bang Bang Ji is the perfect light meal or starter. It's simple to assemble, and you can prepare the chicken and dressing in advance, which makes it an ideal party dish – just increase the quantities for the number of guests.

1. Pour the water into a medium-sized pan, and add the thighs, bones (if you have them), spring onions, ginger, black peppercorns and salt. Bring to the boil over a high heat, and then simmer over a low heat for 12 minutes. Then turn off and leave everything in the liquid for another 5 minutes.

2. To make the dressing, mix the sugar, rice wine vinegar and soy sauce in a medium-sized bowl. Make sure the sugar is dissolved, then add the two oils and black bean sauce. Add the tahini, and then keep the dressing to one side.

3. Take the chicken thighs from the pan and cool them in a bowl of cold water. Save the poaching liquid (see chef's note).

4. Fill a pan with hot water, and cook the beansprouts in it for 1 minute, over a high heat. Drain and cool down in cold water.

5. Take the chicken and beansprouts from the water and pat dry with kitchen paper. Cut the meat into 1cm slices.

6. Arrange the lettuce, tomatoes, cucumber and beansprouts on a large plate. Drizzle the dressing over the top and scatter with the peanuts and spring onions (if you're using them).

Chef's note... You can use the chicken poaching liquid as a stock for various recipes, such as Sichuan Mapo Tofu (see page 18) and Lemak Laksa (see page 92).

Twice-Cooked Pork

Serves 4
5 mins preparation
25 mins cooking

Ingredients

1 star anise
1 cinnamon stick
15 black peppercorns
3 dried goji berries (optional)
300g pork belly, cut in half
600ml water

For the sauce

1 tablespoon chilli bean sauce
1 tablespoon black bean sauce
1 tablespoon miso paste
2 tablespoons Chinese rice wine (Shaoxing) or sake
1 teaspoon white sugar
1 tablespoon soy sauce
2 teaspoons cornflour
4 tablespoons water

For the rest of the dish

1 tablespoon vegetable oil
1 small green pepper, cut into 1-inch squares
300g sweet pointed cabbage, or white cabbage, cut roughly into 1-inch squares
2 garlic cloves, peeled and chopped
1 large onion, peeled and cut into similar size pieces to the green pepper
Chilli oil, if you want to add more spicy heat

Equipment

Medium-sized pan
Large pan
Large wok

Here we use a simple technique to improve the texture and flavour of pork – simmering it in hot water before finishing it in a wok. Similarly, cooking the cabbage and peppers briefly in hot water before frying helps keep their colours nice and bright, and their texture firm. The end result is a sizzling green stir-fry, best served with steamed rice.

1. Put the star anise, cinnamon, peppercorns, goji berries and pork belly in a medium-sized pan. Pour in 600ml of water to cover the meat.

2. Place the large pan over a high heat and bring it to the boil. Then turn down the heat and simmer for 10 minutes.

3. Turn off the heat, but leave the meat in the liquid for 5 more minutes.

4. Meanwhile, in a small bowl, mix the chilli bean sauce, black bean sauce, miso paste, rice wine, sugar and soy sauce. In a separate bowl, mix the cornflour and 4 tablespoons of water.

5. Remove the pork from the pan and let it rest on a plate for 5 minutes. Slice it as thinly as possible, and then keep to one side.

6. Pour 1 litre of hot water from the kettle into a large pan, and put it over a high heat.

7. Place a large wok over the highest heat and add the vegetable oil.

8. Add the green pepper and cabbage to the boiling water. Cook for between 30 seconds and 1 minute, until they change colour slightly, turning brighter. Drain in a colander.

9. Once the wok is hot, add the garlic and fry for 1 minute. Then add the onion, and fry again for another minute.

10. Add the pork and sauce, stirring to coat the meat. Cook for about a minute, and then add the partially cooked cabbage and pepper.

11. When everything has started bubbling, add the cornflour mix to thicken the sauce slightly.

12. Serve on a large plate to share, adding a little chilli oil if you like your food very hot.

Twice-Cooked Pork | 23

Makes about 12 cookies
5 mins preparation
25 mins cooking

Fortune Cookies

These amusing cookies first appeared in the US around 1890 – it's believed a Japanese confectioner introduced them. By World War Two, they were popular in Chinese restaurants, and have been ever since. With some meals, they're all you need at the end – and you have the fun of reading the messages inside. If you make them at home, you can add a personal touch by writing your own messages.

Ingredients

1 egg white
25g caster sugar
30g unsalted butter, melted and cooled slightly
¼ teaspoon almond extract
½ teaspoon vanilla paste
30g pasta flour or plain flour
1 large pinch salt

Equipment

2 baking sheets
2 sheets non-stick baking parchment
Flexible spatula
12-hole muffin tin
12-15 small papers with fortunes (1cm x 5cm)

1. Pre-heat the oven to 180°C/fan 160°C/gas mark 4.

2. In a large bowl, whisk the egg white and sugar lightly, until you have very soft peaks.

3. Add the melted butter, almond extract and vanilla paste, whisking gently. Add the flour and salt, then mix lightly to make a batter.

4. Line 2 baking sheets with non-stick baking parchment. Put a heaped teaspoon of the batter on a sheet and spread it with a flexible spatula. Use an 8cm round cookie cutter as a guide to the size. If the top of the batter looks uneven, level it out with the spatula again.

5. When you've prepared the first 3, bake them in the oven for 5-6 minutes, until the edges are slightly brown.

6. While this first batch of 3 is cooking, prepare the next 3 on the other baking sheet.

7. When the first 3 are cooked, put the next batch in the oven, then work quickly to finish the baked ones, while they're still soft. Place a fortune paper in the middle of one, and fold the cookie in half, pinching the edges to seal, then fold again into a typical fortune cookie shape. Place in the muffin tin to cool. Repeat with the other 2, and then with the next batch of 3, and so on, until you've used all the batter.

8. When the cookies have cooled, put them in an airtight container straight away. They're best eaten on the day you bake them, but will keep for 2-3 days in the container.

JAPANESE

Most of Japan's islands aren't suited to dairy farming or growing cereal crops, but they're really good at producing rice and seafood - so it's no surprise that sushi is the country's most famous dish. But it doesn't stop there - with these recipes, you'll discover the deep, savoury flavours of miso and soy, new ways with fresh vegetables, and irresistible deep-fried family favourites.

27

Serves 4-6
10 mins preparation
15 mins cooking

Crab, Cucumber and Seaweed Salad

Ingredients

1 whole cucumber
1 tablespoon salt
8g wakame seaweed
1 tablespoon lemon juice
120g fresh white crab meat
A few generous pinches of
white pepper
75g samphire (optional)

For the dressing

120ml rice wine vinegar
4 tablespoons white sugar
2 teaspoons soy sauce
4 tablespoons water

To garnish

2 spring onions,
sliced into very thin strips
A few slices of ginger, cut into
thin matchsticks (optional)

Salt-pickled cucumber, seaweed and sweet vinegar dressing are a classic Japanese combination – and adding white crab meat and samphire creates a lovely light lunch or starter. I like to use Cornish or Cromer crab, but fresh crabmeat in a tub is fine too. Or if you prefer to leave out the crab, you'll still have a wonderful salad.

1. Cut the cucumber in half lengthways and scoop out the seeds with a spoon. Slice the cucumber thinly, put the slices in a large bowl and sprinkle with the salt. Mix well with your hands and leave for 10 minutes.

2. Cut the seaweed into 1.5cm lengths and put these in a small bowl. Pour lukewarm water over the seaweed, enough to cover, and leave for 10 minutes.

3. In another small bowl, mix the lemon juice with the crab meat and add the pepper. Keep to one side.

4. Blanch the samphire in boiling water for 1 minute. Drain it, cool in cold water, and then pat dry with kitchen paper.

5. Prepare the dressing by heating the rice wine vinegar and sugar in a small pan until the sugar has dissolved. Add the soy sauce and water, and let it cool.

6. By now, the cucumber should be ready. Using your hands, squeeze out the salty liquid, and put the cucumber in a bowl. Drain the water from the seaweed and lightly squeeze out more water, again using your hands.

7. Add the seaweed and samphire to the cucumber. Pour half of the dressing over and toss well with your hand.

8. Divide individual portions into shallow bowls, and then share the crab between them, placing it on top of each salad. Pour the remaining dressing over and garnish with the spring onions and optional ginger.

Miso and Walnut Aubergine

Serves 4
5 mins preparation
25 mins cooking

Oven-cooked aubergine has a satisfyingly meaty texture. Topped with this sweet miso glaze and chopped walnuts, it makes a delicious starter, suitable for vegetarians and vegans.

Ingredients

2 medium aubergines
1 tablespoon vegetable oil
2 tablespoons brown miso
3 tablespoons mirin
(sweet rice wine)
2 tablespoons sake (rice wine)
or white wine
2 teaspoons granulated
or caster sugar
20g walnuts
1 teaspoon grated ginger

To garnish (optional)

2 spring onions, sliced,
or toasted sesame seeds

Equipment

Large baking tray
Baking parchment
Pastry brush

1. Pre-heat the oven to 190°C/fan 170°C/gas mark 5.

2. Cut the stalks off the aubergines. Using a vegetable peeler peel stripes into the skin from top to bottom, leaving half of the skin in place. Then cut the aubergines into discs, 1.5cm thick.

3. Line a large baking tray with baking parchment and place the aubergine slices on top. Make some 'criss-cross' incisions in the top of each slice, being careful not to cut right through them.

4. Using a pastry brush, smear the vegetable oil over both sides of the aubergine slices. Place them in the oven, and cook for 15 minutes.

5. Spread the walnuts over a small baking sheet and toast them in the oven for 7 minutes. Take them out of the oven and let them cool slightly before chopping them coarsely. Keep to one side.

6. In the meantime, make a miso glaze by combining the miso, mirin, sake (or white wine) and sugar in a small saucepan. Heat until they start to boil, and then turn the heat down and leave to cool slightly.

7. When the aubergine slices look lightly browned, remove them from the oven. Add the grated ginger to the miso glaze and mix thoroughly, then brush the glaze over the tops of the slices and put them back in the oven for 5 minutes.

8. Add the walnuts to the remaining miso glaze and use this to top the aubergine slices. Cook for a further 5 minutes in the oven.

9. Serve hot or warm on individual plates, or on a large plate to share. If you want to garnish with the spring onions or sesame seeds, do this at the last minute.

Chef's note... Serve as individual portions or on a sharing plate.

Pork, Root Vegetable, Tofu and Miso Soup

Serves 4
10 mins preparation
20 mins cooking

Ingredients

1 small onion, peeled
1 small carrot, peeled
100g daikon (sometimes called
mooli, a type of radish), peeled
1 tablespoon vegetable oil
200g pork loin, thinly sliced
50g fresh shiitake mushrooms,
stalks removed, sliced
1 litre water
150g firm tofu,
cut into 1-inch squares
2 tablespoons mirin
(sweet rice wine)
2 tablespoons sake (rice wine)
2 teaspoons soy sauce
1½ tablespoons white sugar
2½ tablespoons miso paste
2 spring onions,
sliced into very thin strips

When I was growing up in Tokyo, this was a favourite winter dish, called 'Tonjiru' in Japanese. The rich broth, with pork, tofu and chunky vegetables, is a really nourishing way to warm up – and if you're vegetarian, it's still very tasty without the pork.

1. Cut the onion into wedges.

2. Slice the carrot, about 5mm thick.

3. Slice the daikon, again about 5mm thick, and then cut each slice into quarters.

4. Heat the oil in a large pan over a medium heat. Add the onion, carrot and daikon, and cook for 3 minutes until they start to turn translucent.

5. Add the pork, and cook until sealed.

6. Add the mushrooms, then pour the water over.

7. Bring the pan to boil and leave to cook over a medium to low heat for 5 minutes. Skim off any solids.

8. Add the tofu, mirin, sake, soy sauce and sugar.

9. Take a ladleful of liquid from the pan and mix it with the miso paste in a small bowl. Add this mixture back to the pan and simmer for 5-10 minutes, or longer if you have time.

10. Check the flavour and add more sugar or miso if necessary. Some miso pastes are saltier than others, so adjust to your taste.

11. Simmer again if you have time and then pour the soup into bowls and sprinkle with the spring onion. Serve while it's warm.

Chef's note... You can keep simmering this soup for 2-3 hours, to give a deeper flavour – and it's even tastier the next day, as all the flavours have time to infuse. If there's any left over, try it with udon noodles.

Tempura Vegetables

Vegetables in Light Batter with Soy Dipping Sauce

Ingredients

120g carrots, peeled and cut into
very thin strips, 5-6cm long
120g sweet potatoes,
cut into 1cm slices
100g aubergine,
cut into 1cm slices
100g sweetcorn
60g green beans
5 fresh shiitake mushrooms,
stalks removed
4 shiso leaves
(optional, see chef's notes)
2-3 litres vegetable oil

For the dipping sauce

60ml sake (rice wine)
60ml mirin (sweet rice wine)
60ml soy sauce
200ml dashi stock
(available from good supermarkets)

To garnish

300g daikon (sometimes called
mooli, a type of radish), finely
grated and with any excess water
squeezed out
4 teaspoons grated ginger

For the batter

1 egg, cold from the fridge
200ml very cold water
115g 00 pasta flour,
sifted a few times

Equipment

Deep fryer or wok

These crispy battered vegetables taste best when they're freshly cooked, and dipped in a tangy sauce. When my mother fried tempura, she kept topping up the large plate at the centre of a table, and didn't sit down with us until it was almost empty. But she didn't go without – she would munch while frying. "Just checking everything's okay," she would say!

1. Put all the prepared vegetables and mushrooms on a tray, ready for frying.

2. Pour the oil into a deep fryer or wok and heat to 180°C.

3. To make the dipping sauce, pour the sake, mirin, soy sauce and dashi into a small pan, placing a lid on top. Leave to simmer keeping the sauce warm.

4. Put the grated daikon and ginger on small individual plates.

5. In a large bowl, mix the egg very lightly with chopsticks. Add the cold water, mix lightly again and then more thoroughly with a whisk. Add flour, one third at a time whilst whisking. Be careful not to over-mix, as the batter can become thick and heavy. Stop when the batter is just mixed.

6. Dip the vegetables in the batter and fry them in batches, draining each batch on kitchen paper. For the carrots and sweetcorn, use a tablespoon to lower them carefully into the oil. Cooking times vary for the different vegetables, but cook them for between 1½ minutes and 2½ minutes – until they float to the top of the oil and become less bubbly, which is usually a sign they're cooked. If you're using shiso leaves, see chef's note below.

7. Divide the dipping sauce into individual bowls. Arrange the tempura on a large plate or small portions on individual plates. Serve hot with the warm dipping sauce and the grated daikon and ginger.

Chef's note... Shiso is a family of basil native in the Far East and South East Asia. Shisho leaves can be found in Asian supermarkets but basil will work as a substitute.

The vegetables don't need coating with flour before dipping in the batter, apart from the shiso leaves. With these, coat only the backs of the leaves with flour, and then dip them in the batter. Cook for 15 seconds.

Serves 4
10 mins preparation
20 mins cooking

Tonkatsu

Crispy Breaded Pork Cutlet

In Japan, there's a superstition about this dish. 'Ton' means pork and 'katsu' means fry. But 'katsu' also means 'to win' – so if someone has an important exam or interview, they might have Tonkatsu for dinner the evening before, to improve their chances. More importantly, with its golden crumb, this pork is wonderfully juicy and crispy, and the recipe also works well with chicken.

Ingredients

4 pork loin slices
Salt and white pepper to season
1 litre vegetable oil
30g plain flour
2 large eggs, lightly beaten
80g panko breadcrumbs

For the sauce

5 tablespoons tomato ketchup
2 tablespoons Worcestershire sauce
1½ tablespoons mirin
(sweet rice wine)
2 tablespoons soy sauce
2 teaspoons white sugar
1 teaspoon mustard powder
½ teaspoon ground ginger
½ teaspoon honey

To serve

1 sweet pointed cabbage,
finely shredded

Equipment

Small jug
Deep fryer or wok
Meat hammer or rolling pin
Salad spinner

1. Crisp up the shredded cabbage by soaking it in a bowl of icy cold water. Keep to one side.

2. Combine all the ingredients for the sauce in a small pan. Cook for 1-2 minutes and then remove from the heat. Pour the sauce into a small jug and leave it to cool.

3. Place the pork slices on a chopping board and cover with cling film. Bash them with a meat hammer or rolling pin to tenderise, then remove the cling film and season with plenty of salt and white pepper.

4. Pour the oil into a deep fryer or wok and heat to 180°C.

5. Coat each pork slice with plain flour, then dip into beaten egg and coat with breadcrumbs. Then put each one back in the egg, and coat again with breadcrumbs. Leave them on a plate until the oil is ready.

6. When the oil is hot, carefully place the pork slices in the fryer or wok, and leave until they become golden. It will take about 5-8 minutes for the meat to cook, depending on the thickness of the slices. If you're using a small fryer or pan, you can do this in batches.

7. While the pork is cooking, drain the cabbage and remove any excess water in a salad spinner, if you have one, or pat dry with a tea towel. Pile the cabbage onto 4 individual plates.

8. When the meat is cooked and golden, lift it out of the oil and drain on few layers of kitchen paper.

9. Transfer the pork to a chopping board, and cut into 1.5cm slices. Arrange these on the plates, next to the cabbage.

10. Drizzle some of the sauce over the cabbage and pork slices. Serve with rice (see page 106).

Chef's note... If you have time after coating the pork slices with breadcrumbs, leave them for 5-10 minutes before frying. This helps make them more golden and crispy.

If you have any sauce left over, you can keep it in the fridge for up to a week.

Teriyaki Salmon with Edamame Rice

Pan-Fried Sweet Soy Salmon Fillet, served with Young Soya Beans, Ginger and Shiso Rice

Ingredients

90ml soy sauce
1 teaspoon honey
1½ tablespoons white sugar
3 tablespoons mirin
(sweet rice wine)
2 tablespoons sake (rice wine)
or white wine
4 fresh salmon fillets
2 tablespoons vegetable oil

For the rice

700g warm cooked rice
(see page 106)
440ml water
3 tablespoons ready-made
sushi vinegar (see page 108)
200g fresh edamame beans
(or frozen ones, thawed)
4 teaspoons lightly toasted white
sesame seeds
1 small handful shiso or basil
leaves, chopped
2 tablespoons sushi pickled
ginger, finely chopped
Salt to season

To garnish

2 spring onions, sliced into very thin
strips and soaked in water (optional)
Extra toasted sesame seeds
3 teaspoons grated ginger

Equipment

Medium-sized pan with a lid
Non-stick frying pan

Teriyaki is probably the best-known Japanese cooking method. It's also very popular, because of its sweet soy sauce flavour. Edamame are young soya beans. Mixed into rice, they add a lovely freshness to this dish, balancing the richness of the salmon.

1. In a small bowl, mix together the soy sauce, honey, sugar, mirin and sake or white wine. Pour into a plastic dish and add the salmon fillets, skin side up. Marinade for 15 minutes.

2. In the meantime, heat a non-stick frying pan and pour in 1 tablespoon of vegetable oil. Take the salmon fillets from the marinade and smear with the remaining oil. Keep the marinade.

3. When the pan is hot, cook the salmon, skin side down, over a medium to high heat – until the skin turns crispy. Turn the fillets over and cook for a more few minutes. Pour the remaining marinade over the fish and turn the heat down to medium low. Cook for a further 5 minutes until the sauce has thickened, using a spoon or pastry brush to keep coating the salmon with the marinade. Keep the salmon in the pre-heated oven (200°C/fan 180°C/gas mark 6) to keep warm until you are ready to serve.

4. Put the cooked rice in a large bowl, mix in the sushi vinegar and add the edamame beans, sesame seeds, shiso (or basil) and chopped pickled ginger. Mix well and season to taste. Divide the rice between 4 individual plates.

5. Finally, place the salmon fillets on the plates and pour over the remaining sauce. Garnish with spring onion, sesame seeds and grated ginger.

Matcha, Lime and Chocolate Tiramisu

Serves 4
30 mins preparation

Ingredients

9g Matcha (green tea powder)
90ml hot water
75g white sugar
1 egg white
½ teaspoon brandy
1 egg yolk
125g mascarpone,
at room temperature
1 tablespoon lime juice
50ml double cream
1 moist chocolate cake loaf
(200g), cut into 5-7mm slices
More Matcha to decorate
Zest of 1 lime, finely grated
Blackberries to decorate (optional)

Equipment

Small hand whisk
Electric whisk

If you go to Japan, you'll see 'Green Sweets', such as sage-green ice cream, forest-green cakes and mint-green latte. They're all flavoured with Matcha green tea, which has been part of our culinary tradition since 800 AD. It's one of my favourite ingredients, and you can try it in this 'east-meets-west' dessert.

1. Put the Matcha powder in a small bowl and pour in the hot water. Mix thoroughly with a whisk, making sure there are no lumps. Add 2 tablespoons of sugar, mix well and leave the syrup to cool.

2. In a large bowl, whisk the egg white and 1 tablespoon of sugar to make meringue. When it's quite stiff, add the brandy.

3. Using a separate bowl, mix the egg yolk, 3 tablespoons of sugar and the mascarpone, until they're thoroughly combined. Add a tablespoon of the Matcha syrup and the lime juice, then mix well again.

4. In another bowl, whip the double cream until it has become stiff and add this to the mascarpone mix.

5. Fold in the meringue and now you're ready to assemble the tiramisu.

6. We want to make four layers. Starting from the bottom: cake, cream, cake, cream. Using a shallow and wide bowl, pour in the Matcha syrup and dip all the cake slices very lightly before lining the bottom of the serving dishes with half of them. Take half of the mascarpone mix and spread it over the cake. Repeat this process, ending up with a layer of mascarpone mix on top. Now you could put the tiramisu in the fridge to rest, or serve it straight away.

7. Just before you serve, sprinkle more Matcha powder over the tiramisu, using a tea strainer. Also scatter with finely grated lime zest. Cut the tiramisu into portions and serve on individual plates, decorated with blackberries (if you're using them).

Chef's note... I used a chocolate cake loaf here, but you could also try this dish with Savoiardi biscuits (lady fingers). You'll need to rest the tiramisu overnight, but this different flavour combination is worth the wait.

Serve as individual portions or in a bowl as a table centre piece, perfect at the end of any meal!

THAI

Much of the food in Thailand is a balance of incredible spicy, sweet and sour flavours, often with chillies and lime. Of course, Thai cooking is very popular here, in the UK, and I couldn't resist including some classics in this section. I hope you enjoy my versions of these, along with the less familiar Thai recipes. Don't miss the mango pudding, one of my all-time favourite desserts.

Serves 4
10 mins preparation
15 mins cooking

Tom Ka Kai

Chicken Coconut Soup

Ingredients

700ml chicken stock
7g galangal,
peeled and thinly sliced
2 lemongrass sticks, cut in half
and bruised with a knife
2 lime leaves
1 red chilli, deseeded and
thinly sliced
400g boneless chicken thighs,
cut into 1-inch cubes
50g shiitake mushrooms,
stalks removed, sliced
1 small handful mangetout,
cut in half
100ml coconut milk
1 teaspoon white sugar
2 teaspoons fish sauce
1 tablespoon lime juice
Salt and white pepper to season

To serve (optional)
Extra red chilli slices
Sliced spring onion
Chopped coriander

In Thailand, this soup is often eaten on hot summer days, but I think it's a lovely way to warm up when the weather turns cold. It blends sweetness with savoury flavours, and a light touch of chilli – that's the warming part! Try it with other starters, like the Fishcakes (see page 50) or Lemongrass Pork Skewers (see page 62).

1. Pour the chicken stock into a large pan. Add the galangal, lemongrass, lime leaves and chilli, and bring to the boil.

2. Add the chicken pieces and mushrooms and continue to cook over a medium heat for 10 minutes.

3. Add the mangetout, coconut milk, sugar and fish sauce and continue cooking for 3 minutes. Taste, and season with salt, pepper or a little extra sugar if necessary.

4. Divide the soup between individual bowls and top with sliced chilli, spring onion and chopped coriander.

Chef's note... If you can't find galangal, you can use ginger slices instead.

Prawn, Squid and Glass Noodle Salad

Ingredients

1 large celery stick, thinly sliced
⅓ cucumber, seeds removed, thinly sliced
1½ teaspoons salt
1 small red onion, thinly sliced
120g green beans
300g mixed seafood, such as baby octopus, squid and tiger prawns
100g mung bean noodles or rice noodles, cooked to the pack instructions, and cooled
160g baby plum tomatoes, halved
1 large lime leaf, finely chopped

For the dressing

2 garlic cloves, finely chopped
1-2 red chillies, seeds removed, finely chopped
40ml lime juice
40ml fish sauce
2 tablespoons white sugar
1 teaspoon soy sauce
1 teaspoon sesame oil
1 small handful of coriander, mint and Thai basil, torn
2 tablespoons chopped plain peanuts

Glass noodles are also called mung bean noodles. As the name suggests, they're translucent. They have a clean, refreshing flavour, so they're well worth looking for – if you can't find them in your supermarket, an oriental grocer will have them. Or you can use rice noodles instead. You'll still have a lovely seafood salad, which you could serve with Pad Thai (see page 48) or Green Curry (see page 54).

1. Cook the noodles, following the instructions on the pack. When cooked, drain and keep to one side.

2. Put the celery and cucumber in a small bowl, and add ½ a teaspoon of salt. Mix lightly with your hands, and leave for 10 minutes.

3. Soak the red onion in a bowl of water for the same length of time, to release some of the bitterness.

4. Bring a small pan of water to the boil. Add ½ a teaspoon of salt and cook the green beans on a medium heat for 5 minutes. Drain, and gently cool down in cold water.

5. Bring another pan of water to the boil. Add ½ a teaspoon of salt and cook the seafood for 2-3 minutes, until it's just cooked through. Drain though a sieve, and cool down in cold water.

6. In a large bowl, combine the noodles, tomatoes and chopped lime leaf, and keep to one side.

7. By now, the cucumber, celery and red onion should be ready. Squeeze out any excess water with your hands and add them to the large bowl.

8. Drain the cooled seafood and beans, pat dry with kitchen paper, and add them to the bowl too.

9. To make the dressing, combine the garlic, red chilli, lime juice, fish sauce, sugar, soy sauce and sesame oil in a small bowl. Mix thoroughly until the sugar has dissolved.

10. Pour the dressing over the salad and mix lightly with your hand. Arrange on a large plate to share, or on individual plates. Pour any remaining dressing from the bottom of the bowl over the top, and sprinkle with coriander, mint, Thai basil and chopped peanuts.

Pad Thai

Stir-Fried Rice Noodles

Classic Pad Thai is a very simple noodle dish, cooked with eggs, prawns, beansprouts and tofu. You can also add a variety of vegetables, making the dish even healthier. I like to do it by the seasons – broccoli in the winter and green beans in the summer.

Ingredients

100g ready to cook rice noodles
1½ tablespoons tamarind paste
1½ tablespoons light brown sugar
1½ tablespoons fish sauce
1½ tablespoons groundnut or vegetable oil
2 garlic cloves, finely chopped
4 shallots, chopped
60g brown shrimps, or North Atlantic prawns
150g firm tofu, cut into small cubes
3 eggs, lightly beaten
1 pinch salt
1 pinch white pepper
240g beansprouts
2 teaspoons light soy sauce
Juice of ½ lime, plus 4 wedges to serve
3 tablespoons roasted, unsalted peanuts, chopped
3 spring onions, sliced into very thin strips
1 small handful of coriander to garnish (optional)
A few pinches of red chilli flakes, to serve

Equipment
Wok

1. Cook the noodles, following the pack instructions. When cooked, drain and keep to one side.

2. Meanwhile, make the Pad Thai sauce by mixing the tamarind paste, sugar and fish sauce in a small bowl. Keep to one side.

3. Heat 1 tablespoon of oil in a wok, on medium to high heat. Add the garlic and shallots and fry for a few minutes before adding the shrimps or prawns, tofu and noodles. Fry for 3 more minutes, then add the Pad Thai sauce, making sure everything is well combined and cooked through.

4. Try one of the noodles to check they have the right texture. If they're a bit too firm, add a few tablespoons of boiling water, stir, check again and repeat if necessary.

5. When you're happy with the noodles, make a hole in the centre, pushing the noodles up the sides of the wok. Pour in the remaining ½ tablespoon of oil and stir in the eggs, with the salt and pepper, and make scrambled eggs. If your wok is not large enough to do this, use another frying pan and make the scrambled eggs, then add it to the noodles.

6. Add the beansprouts, soy sauce and lime juice. Fry for a few minutes, and then arrange the noodles on a large plate or individual plates.

7. Sprinkle with the chopped peanuts, spring onions, coriander, chilli flakes and a lime wedge.

Fishcakes with Sweet Chilli Sauce

Serves 4-6
(makes 12 small fishcakes)
10 mins preparation
20 mins cooking

Ingredients

2 litres vegetable or groundnut oil for deep frying, plus a few extra tablespoons for greasing your hands
400g cod loin, cut into 1-inch chunks
1 egg
2 tablespoons Thai red curry paste
3 tablespoons fish sauce
1 tablespoon white sugar
3 fresh kaffir lime leaves, finely chopped
1 teaspoon sweet paprika
125g green beans, finely sliced
2 spring onions, white part only, finely chopped to serve

To garnish (optional)
Green part of spring onions
Coriander leaves
Lime wedges

To serve
100ml sweet chilli sauce (nuoc cham), see page 61, or a ready-made sweet chilli sauce

Equipment
Deep fryer
Food processor

If you've enjoyed Thai fishcakes in restaurants, you'll love this easy homemade version. The fresh crunch of green beans is a lovely contrast to the soft, spicy fish. And a sweet dipping sauce – whether you make it yourself or buy it – is the perfect accompaniment.

1. Pour the oil into a deep fryer and heat to 170°C.

2. Place the cod chunks in a food processor, and whizz well to make a paste.

3. Put the paste in a large bowl. Add the egg, Thai red curry paste, fish sauce, sugar, chopped kaffir lime leaves, paprika, green beans and spring onions. Mix well to combine thoroughly.

4. Using your hands, divide the mixture into 12. Roll each portion into a small ball, then shape into a flat disc, about 5cm in diameter and 1cm thick. You may find this easier if you use a little oil on your hands, to prevent the paste sticking.

5. When the oil is hot, slide in the fishcakes – you might want to do this in batches, depending on the size of your deep fryer. Cook for 3 minutes, turning occasionally. When they've turned darkish brown, lift them out of the oil and drain on kitchen paper.

6. Arrange the fishcakes on a large plate or individual plates and garnish with sliced spring onions, coriander and lime wedges. Serve with sweet chilli sauce while they're warm.

Green Mango and Papaya Salad

Ingredients

10 cherry tomatoes, halved
2 tablespoons brown shrimps
1 garlic clove, finely chopped
10 green beans, cut in half
3 tablespoons fish sauce
2 bird's eye chillies, stalks removed,
sliced lengthways and deseeded
3 tablespoons lime juice
2 tablespoons light brown sugar
400g green firm mango
and papaya
1 small handful roasted unsalted
peanuts, chopped
Mint and Thai basil to garnish

Equipment

Pestle and mortar

Using fruit in a savoury salad might sound unusual, but this recipe gives you some wonderful flavour combinations. You can also just use mango or papaya – I like the different textures when you put them together. The fruit needs to be quite hard and unripe. If it's too ripe, it might get mashed while you're mixing the salad.

1. Using a pestle and mortar, crush the halved tomatoes, shrimps, garlic and green beans with the fish sauce. Mash them up slightly, and then add the chillies, lime juice and sugar. Taste, and if it's too sour, add more sugar. Mix well and leave for 5 minutes, to let the flavours infuse.

2. Meanwhile, slice the papaya and mango into matchsticks.

3. In a large bowl, mix the papaya and mango with the dressing, and toss well.

4. Remove the chilli slices, and arrange the salad on a large plate or individual plates. Garnish with mint and Thai basil. Serve immediately.

Thai Green Curry

This is one of those dishes that's definitely worth making yourself from scratch. My homemade green curry paste creates much more complex and subtle flavours than anything you can buy in a jar. I've used beef, but this recipe works just as well with chicken or vegetables as an alternative.

Ingredients

1 aubergine,
cut into 1-inch chunks
2 teaspoons salt
1 tablespoon vegetable oil
6 tablespoons green curry paste
300g beef rump steak,
cut into strips
1½ tablespoons fish sauce
2 x 400ml tins coconut milk
2 lime leaves (optional)
2 tablespoons light brown sugar
Juice of 1 lime
1 small handful green beans,
cut in half

For the green curry paste
1 teaspoon coriander seeds
¼ teaspoon caraway seeds
25g shallots,
peeled and cut into quarters
2cm length (about 17g) galangal,
peeled and roughly sliced
2 garlic cloves, peeled
1 lemongrass stick,
roughly chopped
20 green chillies, deseeded
1 lime leaf
Zest of 1 lime
½ tablespoon shrimp paste
½ teaspoon salt
¼ teaspoon white pepper

To garnish (optional)
Thai basil, coriander, red chilli,
spring onions, chopped
Lime wedges

Equipment
Frying pan
Pestle and mortar
Food processor
Wok

1. Place the coriander and caraway seeds in a frying pan, and cook for a few minutes until they're lightly toasted. Crush them using a pestle and mortar, and put them in a small food processor. Add the rest of the green curry paste ingredients and blend until smooth.

2. Put the aubergine chunks in a large bowl, and sprinkle with the salt. Mix with your hands and leave for 5-10 minutes to extract excess moisture.

3. Add the oil to a large wok over a medium to high heat. Fry the curry paste for 1-2 minutes, until it starts to produce a strong aroma.

4. Add the beef strips, and fry until browned.

5. Add the fish sauce, coconut milk, lime leaves and sugar, then bring to the boil.

6. The aubergine should now be ready. Rinse the aubergine thoroughly under running water, drain through a colander and squeeze out the excess water with your hands. Add it to the curry and simmer for 5-10 minutes.

7. Meanwhile, bring a small pan of water to the boil and cook the green beans for a few minutes. Drain and add to the curry.

8. Arrange the curry in bowls or on plates, and garnish with your choice of herbs. Serve with cooked jasmine rice or Thai sticky rice.

Serves 4-6

5 mins preparation
25 mins cooking

Mango Pudding with Lime Syrup

Ingredients

6 sheets gelatine
690ml water
3 tablespoons hot water
6 tablespoons white sugar
1 tablespoon lime juice
450ml sweetened Alphonso
mango purée (see chef's note)
6 tablespoons evaporated milk

For the syrup

4 tablespoons milk or water
3 tablespoons white sugar
6 tablespoons evaporated milk
2 tablespoons lime juice

To serve

Sprigs of mint
1 fresh mango, sliced

Equipment

4-6 small jelly moulds (around
100ml, see chef's note)
1 small microwavable bowl

Mangoes are hugely popular all over South East Asia –
especially in Thailand, where you'll often see fresh mango
slices served with sticky rice. The other popular way it's eaten
is this sweet, creamy pudding. I love it with lime syrup poured
over, making it even creamier.

1. In a jug or bowl, add the gelatine sheets to 600ml water and soak for
   5 minutes.

2. Squeeze the water out with your hands, and place the gelatine in a small
   microwavable bowl. Add 90ml of water and put cling film over the bowl.
   Microwave on full power for 10 seconds. Make sure the gelatine has dissolved
   – if not, give it 5 more seconds.

3. Combine 3 tablespoons of hot water with the sugar, making sure the sugar
   dissolves completely. Then add the lime juice and pour into the gelatine mix,
   stirring well.

4. Pour ¾ of the mango purée into a bowl, adding the remaining quarter to
   the sugar and gelatine mix, and pour back into the bowl of mango purée.

5. Add the evaporated milk and mix thoroughly. Divide the mixture between
   4 jelly moulds.

6. Place the moulds in a deep container, large enough to take all four. Put
   crushed ice and cold water around the moulds, and place the container in the
   fridge. The gelatine should be set in about 20-25 minutes. (See chef's note.)

7. Meanwhile, to make the syrup, pour the milk or water into a small
   microwavable bowl and put cling film over the top. Microwave on full power
   for 10 seconds, and then add the sugar. Stir to dissolve the sugar, and then
   add the evaporated milk. Leave to cool slightly and then add the lime juice,
   stirring frequently with a small whisk to avoid curdling.

8. To check whether the puddings are ready, touch the tops lightly – they
   shouldn't stick to your finger.

9. Dip the moulds in hot water for 2-3 seconds, and turn out the puddings
   onto plates. Pour the lime syrup over the top, and decorate each one with
   a sprig of mint and sliced fresh mango.

Chef's note... You can usually find tins of mango purée in the Asian aisle of supermarkets.

If you're making the pudding in advance, you can chill it in the fridge without the ice
and water, for 3-4 hours, or simply leave in the fridge overnight to set.

Whether you use 4, 5 or 6 jelly moulds depends on their size. If you put more than
around 100ml of liquid in each one, they'll take longer to set.

VIETNAMESE

Just after daybreak in Ho Chi Minh City, thousands of rickety shacks and street corners become makeshift cafés, created by families who bring everything with them – from cooking pots to plastic stools for their customers. The food they serve is light, fresh and fragrant. It's like culinary heaven on the pavement! Here are some Vietnamese favourites to try in the comfort of your own kitchen.

Serves 4

Fresh Summer Rolls

Ingredients

100g pork belly
6 large tiger prawns, peeled
50g rice vermicelli noodles
4 rice papers (20-22cm)
6-8 leaves round lettuce or soft
leaf lettuce
4 sprigs fresh mint
4 sprigs coriander
4 shiso or Thai basil leaves
8 stalks chives, or Chinese chives
¼ cucumber, core removed and
cut into matchsticks
1 carrot, peeled and sliced into
very thin strips

For the sweet chilli sauce
(nuoc cham)
(Makes about 100ml)
30g white sugar, diluted with
45ml cold water
3 tablespoons lime juice
2 tablespoons fish sauce
2 garlic cloves,
peeled and finely chopped
2 red chillies,
deseeded and finely chopped
Salt to season

To garnish
Chopped mint, coriander
and chives

Unlike spring rolls, summer rolls aren't fried in oil, so they're much lighter. They're very simple to make – salad, herbs, pork and prawns, wrapped in rice paper and served with a sweet chilli dipping sauce, known as 'nuoc cham'. If you're short of time, you can make this recipe even easier by buying a ready-made sweet chilli sauce.

1. Place the pork belly in a small pan and cover with water. Bring to the boil and then simmer for 10 minutes. Leave in the hot water for 5 minutes, then remove from the pan and leave to cool down slightly.

2. Cook the prawns in boiling salted water for 1-2 minutes, until they change colour. Drain and cool under running water. Slice each prawn in half.

3. Cook the rice vermicelli noodles, following the instructions on the pack. Cool under running water, drain and keep to one side.

4. Take the pork, and slice the thick layer of meat as thinly as possible, discarding the fat.

5. In a large bowl or container, soak the rice papers in water for a few seconds, and then place them on a clean, wet tea towel. On the first rice paper, line up three prawns, with a quarter of the lettuce, pork, noodles, herbs, cucumber and carrots, along the edge closest to you. Using both hands, start rolling away from you, folding in the sides. When you've made your first roll, put it on a plate and cover with another wet tea towel, to stop it drying out. Repeat with the other three rice papers.

6. To make the sweet chilli sauce, combine all the ingredients apart from the garlic and red chilli. Make sure the sugar has dissolved completely, and then add the garlic and chilli. Season with salt to taste, and then pour it into individual dipping bowls.

7. Arrange the rolls on a plate and garnish with extra herbs. Serve immediately with the dipping sauce.

Chef's note... If you're vegetarian or vegan, you could make these rolls without the pork and prawns, perhaps replacing them with thinly sliced red pepper, shredded firm mango or tofu. In the dipping sauce, use soy sauce instead of fish sauce.

Lemongrass Pork Skewers

Pork Meatballs on Lemongrass Skewers

Ingredients

12 lemongrass sticks
400g minced pork
4 spring onions, finely chopped
5 garlic cloves, peeled and
finely chopped
4 teaspoons cornflour
2 tablespoons fish sauce
1 teaspoon white sugar
A large pinch of white pepper
1 tablespoon lard
1 tablespoon vegetable oil

To garnish (optional)

Small bunch of coriander
Lime wedges
Thai basil or mint

Chilli dressing (optional)

3 tablespoons Sriracha
chilli sauce
½ garlic clove, grated
½ teaspoon sugar
2 tablespoons water

Equipment

Baking tray

Using lemongrass sticks as skewers is a speciality of northern Vietnamese and Cambodian cooking. The aromatic lemongrass infuses citrusy flavours into the pork as it cooks, adding great complexity and freshness to the dish.

1. Pre-heat the oven to 220°C/fan 200°C/gas mark 7.

2. To prepare the lemongrass, make a cut 1cm up from the bottom of each stick, about 7cm in length. Wrap the sticks in wet kitchen paper and microwave on high for 2 minutes. Put on one side to cool down.

3. Put the minced pork in a large bowl, and add the spring onions, garlic, cornflour, fish sauce, sugar, white pepper and lard. Mix well with your hands and divide the mixture into 12 oval-shaped balls. Wet your hands with water if you need to.

4. Make an additional incision on the other side of the lemongrass, making four sections. Repeat the same to other lemongrass.

5. Take each meat portion and thread it onto a lemongrass skewer. Don't worry if they look slightly messy at first – you can reshape them as you go (again, using wet hands will make this easier).

6. Place the skewers on a baking tray, and brush with a thin layer of oil. Cook them in the oven for 15 minutes, turning once halfway through the cooking time.

7. Serve on a large plate or individual plates, with garnishes such as coriander, lime wedges, Thai basil or mint. If you like your skewers extra spicy, you could also add a chilli dressing – simply mix Sriracha sauce with the grated garlic and water.

Rare Beef Pho

Fragrant Broth with Rice Noodles, Herbs and Sliced Beef

Ingredients

200g dried rice noodles, about 5mm width
1 star anise
2 cardamom pods, crushed
½ cinnamon stick
4 shallots, skins on, quartered
4 garlic cloves, crushed
2 teaspoons vegetable oil
4 large slices of ginger
2 teaspoons black peppercorns
2 spring onions, roughly chopped
1.2 litres organic beef stock (either freshly made or diluted stock cubes)
½ teaspoon white sugar
1 lime leaf
1 teaspoon fish sauce
Salt and white pepper to season
200g beef fillet, finely sliced
½ onion, finely sliced and soaked in water
100g beansprouts
1 bird's eye chilli, finely sliced
4 lime wedges
2 spring onions, finely sliced
1 handful chopped coriander, mint, shiso or Thai basil

Pho is a dish of rice noodles in a light, fragrant broth made with chicken, beef or pork stock. In Vietnam, it's a popular street food, served at breakfast time. Here I've turned it into an evening meal, by using beef stock, and topping it off with a few slices of tender rare fillet.

1. Pre-heat the oven to 240°C/fan 220°C/gas mark 9.

2. Place the rice noodles in a large bowl and pour enough warm water over to cover them. Leave for 20-25 minutes, until the noodles are fairly soft.

3. Place the star anise, cardamom pods and cinnamon stick on a small metal baking tray, and dry roast them in the oven for 3 minutes.

4. Put the shallots and garlic on a separate baking tray, and smear with oil. Cook in the oven for 10 minutes.

5. Meanwhile, transfer the roasted spices to a large pan, and add the ginger, black peppercorns, roughly cut spring onions and beef stock. Bring to the boil on the highest heat.

6. When the shallots and garlic are soft, add them to the pan. Turn down the heat and simmer gently for 5-10 minutes.

7. Pour the broth through a sieve to remove the spices. Discard the spices and pour the liquid back in the pan. Simmer again on a low heat and add the sugar, fish sauce and lime leaf. Taste, and, if necessary, adjust the flavour by adding a little more fish sauce or a pinch of salt. Season with white pepper.

8. Drain the noodles and cook them in the broth for 1-2 minutes, until they're soft enough to eat. Divide them between the 4 warmed bowls.

9. Put the fillet slices on top of the noodles, and pour the piping hot broth over. Arrange the onion slices, beansprouts, chilli slices, lime wedges and spring onions on each bowl, and scatter with plenty of green herbs. Eat while it's hot.

Serves 4

Grilled Pork and Rice Noodles

Ingredients

For the marinade
2 shallots, finely chopped
2 tablespoons white sugar
2 teaspoons fish sauce
2 teaspoons ketjap manis
(available from oriental grocery
shops and some supermarkets)
or soy sauce
A few pinches of white pepper

400g pork loin, fat and rind
removed and thinly sliced
1 tablespoon vegetable oil

For the daikon and carrot sweet pickle
100g daikon (sometimes called
mooli, a type of radish), peeled
and cut into matchsticks
2 carrots, peeled and cut
into 5cm matchsticks
½ tablespoon salt
1½ tablespoons white sugar
1 tablespoon rice wine vinegar

For the rest of the recipe
200g rice noodles
160g lettuce leaves
1 small handful of coriander, mint,
shiso leaves and Thai basil
4 tablespoons crushed peanuts
8 spring rolls (shop bought),
cooked according to pack
instructions

To serve
Nuoc cham dipping sauce (see
page 61) or 100ml ready-made
sweet chili sauce diluted with
60ml water

I love this dish after a long day at work – it's light and tasty, and quick to make. Thin rice noodles with plenty of vegetables, herbs, marinated pork and chilli sauce. Lots of flavours, ready in very little time.

1. Put the daikon, carrots, ½ tablespoon salt and ½ tablespoon sugar in a bowl. Mix lightly with your hands and leave for 5 minutes. Mix again, and leave for another 5 minutes.

2. In another bowl, mix all the ingredients for the marinade and add the meat. Leave for 10 minutes.

3. If there is any water coming out of the carrots and daikon, pour away and rinse them under running water, then drain and squeeze with your hand. Put the remaining tablespoon of sugar and the rice wine vinegar in a clean bowl. Add the daikon and carrots, mix well, and leave to pickle for 5 minutes.

4. Remove the pork from the marinade. Add the oil to a frying pan, and stir-fry the meat for 5 minutes, until it's slightly browned and any liquid has gone.

5. Cook the rice noodles, following the instructions on the pack. Drain and divide between 4 individual bowls.

6. On top of the noodles, arrange some lettuce leaves, coriander, mint, shiso leaves and Thai basil. Then add the cooked pork and crushed peanuts, and serve with spring rolls and nuoc cham or sweet chili sauce. This dish is best served warm.

Chef's note... If you have more time for pickling the daikon and carrots, add 150ml water after the second pickling stage (with the rice vinegar). Leave for 6 hours or overnight.

| Fried Whole Sea Bream with Garlic, Tamarind and Chilli Sauce

Fried Whole Sea Bream with Garlic, Tamarind and Chilli Sauce

Ingredients

2 litres vegetable oil for deep frying
2 x sea bream or snapper, cleaned and scaled
1 tablespoon vegetable oil
2 tablespoons finely chopped shallots
4 garlic cloves, peeled and finely chopped
2 teaspoons chopped red chilli
1 tablespoon finely chopped lemongrass
2 teaspoons tamarind paste, diluted with 100ml water
1½ tablespoons Thai fish sauce
2 tablespoons granulated sugar
1 teaspoon cornflour, mixed with 30ml water
Salt to season
75g rice flour

To garnish (optional)

Thinly sliced spring onions
Sliced red chillies
Coriander, roughly chopped
Lime wedges

Equipment

Deep fryer or large wok
Frying pan

Sea Bream has such a delicate texture and it's easy to eat off the bone – but if you prefer to use fillets, this recipe still works well. You could also try it with snapper, which is one of my favourite fish. Either way, you'll have succulent white meat and crispy skin, all drizzled with a spicy, garlicky sauce.

1. Pour the oil into a deep fryer or large wok and heat to 170°C.

2. Wash the fish inside and out, and pat dry with kitchen paper. Make 3 diagonal cuts on each side of the fish.

3. In a frying pan, heat 1 tablespoon of vegetable oil, and fry the shallots, garlic, red chilli and lemongrass over a high heat for a few minutes. When the aromas start to rise from the pan, add the diluted tamarind paste, fish sauce, sugar and cornflour. Stir thoroughly until the sauce thickens slightly. Taste, and season with salt if necessary. Keep to one side.

4. Dust the fish with rice flour and slide it slowly into the deep fryer or wok. If you're using 2 smaller fish, fry them for about 4 minutes. For a large fish, cook for 6-7 minutes. When it turns light brown, it should be ready. Remove it carefully from the oil and place on a large plate.

5. Warm up the sauce, adding a few tablespoons of water if it's too thick. Pour it over the fish, and garnish with spring onions, chillies, coriander and lime. Serve with steamed rice or noodles.

Chef's note... This is quite a hot dish, if you prefer a milder sauce, add less chopped chillies.

Seabass, snapper or bream fish can be used.

Vietnamese Savoury Pancakes

Ingredients

250g pork belly, fat and rind
removed and cut into 1cm slices
A few pinches of salt
3 tablespoons vegetable oil
1 small onion, finely sliced
150g cooked tiger prawns
Salt and pepper to season
100g beansprouts
2 spring onions, finely sliced

For the pancake batter

40g rice flour
10g plain flour
¼ teaspoon turmeric
25ml coconut milk
125ml water
A large pinch of salt

To serve

1 small bunch of chopped Thai
basil or basil, mint, coriander
and shiso leaves
1 small soft lettuce
Nuoc cham sweet chilli dipping
sauce (see page 61)

Equipment

Non-stick frying pan with a lid

I like to roll these pancakes in lettuce leaves, like a wrap, and eat them with my fingers. The pork, prawn and onion filling is incredibly tasty, and goes perfectly with the sweet chilli dipping sauce. A fun, informal starter.

1. Pour about 1 litre of water into a large pan. Add a few large pinches of salt and the pork belly slices. Bring to the boil and simmer for 7 minutes.

2. Meanwhile, mix together all the pancake batter ingredients in a bowl, and keep to one side.

3. When the pork is cooked, drain it through a sieve and cool it down under running water for 3 minutes. Drain it again and pat dry with kitchen paper. Slice thinly and keep to one side.

4. Heat a tablespoon of oil in a non-stick frying pan. When it's hot, add the sliced onion, pork and prawns, and season lightly with salt and pepper. Fry for a few minutes until prawns are heated through, and then transfer to a plate.

5. Using the same pan, heat another tablespoon of oil. Stir the batter mix well, and pour half of it into the pan. Tilt the pan to spread the batter evenly, making a thin, round pancake.

6. Reduce the heat and sprinkle on half of the beansprouts, spring onions, prawns and pork. Season with salt and pepper. Place a lid on the pan, and cook for 2 minutes, until the beansprouts are done.

7. Continue cooking for another 5-7 minutes on a low heat, until the edge of the pancake starts turning light brown and the middle of the pancake looks fairly dry. Check the bottom of the pancake. If it's a golden colour, fold it into a semi-circle and place it on a plate, keep it warm.

8. Repeat steps 5, 6 and 7 for more pancakes.

9. Garnish with the herbs, and serve with lettuce leaves and sweet chilli sauce.

15 mins preparation
15 mins cooking

Sweet Sesame Mini Doughnuts

Sesame doughnuts are widely popular across the Far East and South East Asia. They're usually made from rice flour and filled with sweet bean paste. I prefer to use wheat flour for a more familiar doughy texture, and to make a sticky sesame filling. Wonderful with Vietnamese coffee or jasmine tea.

Ingredients

1 tablespoon caster sugar
1½ teaspoons fast-acting yeast
50ml warm water
70g strong bread flour
50g plain flour
20g cornflour
¼ teaspoon salt
1 litre vegetable or groundnut oil
for deep frying
60ml lukewarm water
3 tablespoons white
sesame seeds

For the sesame filling

4 tablespoons toasted white
sesame seeds
3½ tablespoons white sugar
½ tablespoon cornflour
4 tablespoons coconut milk
¼ teaspoon soy sauce
A few generous pinches of salt

Equipment

Deep fryer or wok
Small spice grinder/pestle
and mortar

1. Combine the caster sugar and yeast in a small bowl. Add 50ml warm water and leave for 5 minutes, until the mixture becomes frothy.

2. Meanwhile, mix the strong bread flour, plain flour, cornflour and salt in a large bowl and place to one side.

3. Pour the oil into a deep fryer or wok and heat to 160°C.

4. To make the filling, grind the toasted sesame seeds in a small spice grinder or pestle and mortar. Add 3½ tablespoons of sugar, and grind until you have a fine powder. Put the cornflour and coconut milk in a small saucepan, and stir well over a medium to low heat for a few minutes, using a spatula. Keep stirring until it's a thick mayonnaise consistency, and then place in a small bowl and stir in the sugar and sesame mix, soy sauce and salt.

5. Add the sugar and yeast mixture to the flour mixture, and add 60ml of lukewarm water. Mix to make the dough, adding a little more water if it's too dry. Turn onto a floured surface and knead for a few minutes.

6. Divide the dough into 8 balls. Taking each one in turn, use your finger to poke a hole in the centre, and insert 1½ teaspoons of the sesame paste. Pinch the edges of the dough to seal the end, making sure there are no holes.

7. Lightly wet the doughnuts with your hands, and dunk each one in a bowl of white sesame seeds, using a spoon to coat them evenly.

8. Fry the doughnuts in the hot oil for 2-3 minutes, turning them regularly. When they've turned golden brown, remove them carefully from the oil and drain on kitchen paper. You'll probably need to do this in batches, depending on the size of your fryer or wok.

9. Leave the doughnuts to cool for 2-5 minutes.

Chef's note... You could try different fillings, such as sweet chestnut paste (sold in supermarkets). Or you could make the sesame paste using black sesame seeds – they have a stronger flavour, so you'll need to add another tablespoon of sugar.

KOREAN

Red chillies, sesame oil and garlic combine deliciously to create the trademark flavours of Korean cooking. Pickling and fermenting are also popular, adding a tangy, slightly salty taste to side dishes. The most famous is kimchi – I've included a quick version here, among a variety of dishes you may never have tried before, but will definitely want to enjoy again!

Quick Kimuchi

Hot Chinese Cabbage

Ingredients

400g Chinese cabbage, cut into
1cm strips
100g carrots, cut into matchsticks
30g coarse salt
2 garlic cloves, peeled and
roughly chopped
2cm piece of ginger
½ small onion, peeled and roughly
chopped
1½ tablespoons fish sauce
2 tablespoons Korean chilli flakes
(see chef's note)
½ teaspoon honey
1 teaspoon brown sugar
1 bird's eye chilli, deseeded and
chopped finely
Sesame seeds and spring onions
to garnish (optional)

Equipment
Small food processor

In a traditional Korean kitchen, a jar of Chinese cabbage, salted and fermented with fish sauce and chilli, would take a few weeks to mature. With this quick version, you can have all those exciting flavours and textures ready in 30 minutes. Try it with a bowl of rice, miso soup and nori seaweed, or eaten as a side with grilled meat and fish.

1. Add the salt to 1 litre of water in a pan, over a high heat. Let the water boil for a few minutes to dissolve the salt, add the cabbage and carrots making sure they're fully covered and leave to soak for 15 minutes, mixing once halfway through.

2. Place the garlic, ginger, onion, fish sauce, chilli flakes, honey and sugar in a small food processor and whizz until you have a smooth paste.

3. When the cabbage and carrots have finished soaking, drain them in a colander, then rinse in cold running water. Squeeze with your hands to remove excess water, and place in a clean bowl.

4. Mix your chilli paste into the vegetables, and add the bird's eye chilli. Mix again, and they're ready to serve, garnished with sesame seeds and spring onions – or you can put them in a sterilised jar in the fridge and eat any time within a week.

Chef's note... Korean chilli flakes are fairly mild. If you can't find them, you could use Turkish red pepper flakes instead – but don't use other types of chilli powder, such as cayenne, or chilli flakes, as they could make the dish too hot to eat.

It's the bird's eye chilli that gives this recipe its heat. If you prefer a milder flavour, leave it out.

Chive and Seafood Pancakes

Serves 4

10 mins preparation
15 mins cooking

Ingredients

140g plain flour
1 teaspoon cornflour
⅓ organic chicken stock cube, diluted with 50ml hot water
1 teaspoon miso paste, diluted with 2 tablespoons hot water
1 egg
120ml water
20g chives, cut into 5cm lengths
8 spring onions, cut into 5cm lengths, white parts sliced in half
½ small onion, thinly sliced
150g mixed seafood (such as squid, clams and prawns), roughly chopped
1½ tablespoons groundnut oil

For the dipping sauce

2 tablespoons soy sauce
1 teaspoon white sugar
½ tablespoon rice wine vinegar
2 tablespoons water
1 teaspoon sesame oil

Equipment

Non-stick frying pan

When I was studying in London nearly 20 years ago, I had a Korean classmate. One day, we had a small party, making something we usually eat at home – and she made these pancakes. She was very enthusiastic about their flavour and texture, and I'm so glad she gave me the recipe which I can share with you.

1. Combine the plain flour and cornflour in a large bowl.

2. Make up the stock into a measuring jug and add the diluted miso paste, egg and 120ml of water. In total, this should be around 200ml or a little more.

3. Add the liquid mixture to the flour and use a whisk to mix thoroughly.

4. Put the chives, spring onions, sliced onion and seafood into the batter, and mix well with a fork or chopsticks.

5. This pancake batter is enough for two batches, so divide it in half.

6. Place a non-stick frying pan over a medium to high heat, and pour in the groundnut oil. When it's hot, pour in half of the batter and cook for 4-5 minutes. Adjust the heat if necessary to make sure the pancake doesn't burn on the bottom (we're aiming for golden brown). Turn it over and cook the other side for 4-5 minutes, pressing well to keep it flat. If you want to be absolutely sure it's evenly cooked, you can flip it a few times. When it's done, put it on a warm plate and cut into 8 pieces.

7. Repeat with the other half of the batter.

8. Make the dipping sauce by mixing together all the ingredients. Divide this between 4 small bowls, sprinkle with sesame seeds and chilli slices, and serve with the warm pancakes.

Chef's note... For vegetarians or vegans, use vegetable stock instead of chicken stock and leave out the seafood. With the chives and onions, the pancakes are still extremely tasty.

Namul

Seasoned Vegetables

Ingredients

1 cucumber, seeds removed,
sliced into strips
3 teaspoons salt
1 teaspoon white sugar
4 carrots, peeled and cut into
matchsticks
10g dried wakame seaweed,
soaked in lukewarm water
300ml water
250g beansprouts
4 teaspoons sesame oil
2 teaspoons grated garlic
1 teaspoon sesame seeds
200g shiitake mushrooms, stalks
removed, sliced
2 teaspoons soy sauce

Equipment
Scissors

Korean people love their vegetable dishes. Namul can include all kinds of combinations, sautéed with sesame oil, garlic and seasonings. Here I've used cucumber, carrots, seaweed, beansprouts and mushrooms – try it with Bibimbap (see page 82) or Gimbap (see page 84).

1. Place the cucumber strips in a small bowl with 1½ teaspoons of the salt and 1 teaspoon of sugar. Put the carrots sticks in a separate bowl, and add ½ teaspoon of salt. Mix the contents of each bowl with your hands, and leave for 5-10 minutes.

2. Drain the wakame seaweed, squeeze it lightly and cut into 2-3cm strips with a pair of scissors. Keep it to one side.

3. In a large pan, boil 300ml of water with 1 teaspoon of salt. Add the beansprouts and leave to cook for 1 minute, and then drain through a sieve.

4. Pat the beansprouts dry with kitchen paper and put them in a bowl. Add 1 teaspoon of the sesame oil and ½ a teaspoon of the grated garlic. Toss well and leave to cool on a metal baking sheet.

5. Now the cucumber and carrots should be ready for further cooking. Squeeze out the excess water with your hands.

6. For the carrots, heat a small frying pan with ½ a teaspoon of the sesame oil and ½ a teaspoon of the grated garlic. When they start to sizzle, add the carrot slices and fry for 1 minute. Put them on the baking sheet to cool down.

7. Repeat this process for the cucumber.

8. For the wakame seaweed, it's very similar. Add 1 teaspoon of sesame oil to a pan with ½ a teaspoon of grated garlic and 1 teaspoon of soy sauce. When they're sizzling, add the wakame seaweed and fry for 1 minute before transferring to a metal baking sheet. Sprinkle with the sesame seeds and leave to cool down.

9. Similar again for the shiitake mushrooms. Heat 1 teaspoon of sesame oil and fry the mushrooms until they're slightly brown. Add 1 teaspoon of soy sauce, stir, and leave to cool down on the baking sheet.

10. Once all the vegetables are cool, arrange them in individual bowls and serve with meat or fish dishes.

Chef's note... To save time preparing the cucumber and carrots, a vegetable slicer comes in very handy. A garlic press or fine grater makes life easier, too.

Bibimbap

One Bowl Meal with Rice, BBQ Beef, Seasoned Vegetables and Gochujang Sauce

This healthy one-bowl meal consists of marinated beef, namul (seasoned vegetables, see page 81), rice, and a poached or fried egg. The traditional Korean method involves putting raw eggs, beef and vegetables in stone bowls so hot they cook everything. My version simply uses a frying pan!

Ingredients

For the marinade
2 tablespoons light soy sauce
2 teaspoons white sugar
2 teaspoons sesame oil
2 teaspoons rice wine
2 shallots, peeled and roughly chopped
2 garlic cloves, crushed
1 teaspoon sesame seeds

300g beef fillet, very thinly sliced

For the gochujang sauce
4 tablespoons gochujang (Korean chilli paste)
4 teaspoons light brown sugar
4 teaspoons sesame oil
80ml water

For the rest of the recipe
4 eggs
2 tablespoon vegetable oil
700g cooked short grain or sushi rice, still hot (see page 106)

To serve
Selection of namul (see page 81)
Toasted sesame seeds for garnish (optional)

1. In a large bowl, combine all the marinade ingredients, adding the beef last. Make sure all the beef slices are well coated, cover with cling film and leave in the fridge for 15 minutes.

2. To make the gochujang sauce, mix the gochujang, brown sugar, sesame oil and water in a small bowl. Divide between 4 small individual bowls and keep to one side.

3. Heat the oil in a clean frying pan, on medium to high heat. Fry the beef slices for about 5 minutes, or until they turn brown. Reduce the heat and leave to cook for a few more minutes.

4. Meanwhile, heat another non-stick frying pan, and fry the eggs to suit your preference. Divide the hot cooked rice between 4 large individual bowls. Place the namul on top, then the beef, followed by an egg on top of each bowl. Sprinkle with sesame seeds and pour the gochujang sauce over. Stir in the sauce as you eat.

Chef's note... For vegetarians, the same marinade works very nicely with soy-based meat replacements or Quorn.

Gimbap

Korean Sushi Rolls

Ingredients

50g apple or pear, peeled, cored
and cut into small chunks
½ small onion, peeled,
cut into small chunks
2 garlic cloves, peeled
1cm ginger
1½ tablespoons soy sauce
1 tablespoon brown sugar
A few large pinches of salt
1 teaspoon sesame oil
200g beef steak (sirloin or rump),
thinly sliced

For the rest of the recipe

550g cooked sushi rice, still hot
(see page 106)
3 teaspoons sesame oil
1 tablespoon sesame seeds
½ teaspoon salt,
plus extra to season
200g fresh spinach leaves
100g carrot, peeled and sliced
into very thin strips
½ teaspoon soy sauce
1 teaspoon vegetable oil
½ garlic clove, grated
¼ cucumber, seeds removed,
thinly sliced
4 nori seaweed sheets, cut into
21cm x 15cm rectangles

Equipment

Food processor
2 microwavable bowls
Bamboo sushi rolling mat
(many supermarkets sell these)

As a child, I loved Japanese sushi rolls at picnics or on school trips. Gimbap is the Korean version – a roll of seasoned rice with fillings of vegetables, fish or meat, wrapped in nori seaweed paper. In this recipe, I use marinated beef. If you want a vegetarian version, you can use soya mince instead (fry it until it's fairly dry).

1. In a food processor, blend all the marinade ingredients, apart from the beef. Place the beef in a large bowl, pour the marinade over and leave for 10 minutes.

2. Place the hot cooked rice in a bowl, and stir in the 2 teaspoons of sesame oil, along with the sesame seeds and ½ a teaspoon of salt. Leave to cool down.

3. Take 2 microwavable bowls, and put the spinach leaves in one and the carrots in the other. Add about 50ml of water to each, and cover with cling film.

4. Cook the spinach in a microwave on full power, for 1½ minutes. When it's cooked, cool it down under running water and drain through a sieve. Squeeze out as much water as possible with your hands, and mix in the soy sauce.

5. Microwave the carrots on full power for 2 minutes, and drain through a sieve. Place a frying pan over a medium heat. Add the oil, and then stir-fry the carrots with the garlic for 1 minute. Leave to cool down on a metal tray.

6. Heat the remaining sesame oil in a frying pan and cook the beef and marinate for 5-6 minutes on a medium heat. (Cool down slightly on a metal tray).

7. Place one sheet of nori seaweed on a bamboo rolling mat, with the longer side facing towards you. Spread a quarter of the rice over the nori seaweed, leaving an inch gap to one end on the long side. You may need to sprinkle a little water on the rice, to make it easier to spread.

8. Lay a quarter of the spinach, carrot, cucumber and beef on top of the rice. Starting with the side of the nori opposite the end with no rice, carefully lift up the mat and nori, fold in the fillings, and then roll up. When you've made the roll, leave it in the bamboo mat for 5 minutes – this helps the nori stick together and makes it easier to slice.

9. Repeat steps 6 and 7 for the other rolls.

10. Cut each roll into 8 pieces, and serve with soy dipping sauce (see page 78) or plain soy sauce.

Chef's note... You can also cook the spinach and carrots by boiling in salted water. I've just suggested the microwave here to speed things up.

Crispy Fried Chicken

Ingredients

800g chicken wings
(or 700g chicken thighs)
2 tablespoons white or red wine
½ teaspoon grated ginger
¼ teaspoon grated garlic
¼ teaspoon sea salt
60g cornflour
½ tablespoon baking powder
1 litre vegetable or groundnut oil

For the sauce

1½ tablespoons soy sauce
4 tablespoons mirin (sweet rice
wine) or sake (rice wine)
2½ tablespoons rice wine vinegar
1½ tablespoons gochujang
(Korean chilli paste)
3 tablespoons honey
3 teaspoons sesame oil
2 tablespoons light brown sugar
1 teaspoon grated ginger

To serve (optional)

A few handfuls of peanuts, or
toasted sesame seeds
Salad leaves

Equipment

Deep fryer or wok
Another wok or large frying pan

Just as children in the UK might spend some of their pocket money in the local chippy, Korean kids like to buy 'Dakgangjeong'. It's crispy fried chicken with a sticky, sweet and spicy coating. Try making it for your own boys and girls – I'm sure they'll love it!

1. Put all the chicken pieces in a large bowl and add the wine, ginger and garlic. Mix well with your hands and leave for at least 5 minutes.

2. Combine the salt, cornflour and baking powder in a bowl, mix well with a spoon.

3. Add the flour mix to the chicken, and use your hands to make sure the chicken is well coated. Arrange the pieces on a plate or baking tray.

4. Pour the oil into a deep fryer or wok and heat to 180°C.

5. While the oil is heating, make the sauce by mixing all the ingredients in a small bowl. (You can make the sauce in advance, and keep it in the fridge for up to a week.)

6. When the oil is hot, carefully lower in the chicken pieces and fry until they turn golden. If you want to do this in batches, drain each batch on kitchen paper and keep it warm while you do the rest.

7. Once all the chicken is cooked, put the sauce into a large, clean wok or frying pan over a medium heat. When it starts to bubble, add the crispy fried chicken, and coat it evenly with the sticky sweet sauce.

8. Top with peanuts or toasted sesame seeds, and serve with salad leaves.

Hotteok

Sweet Griddled Pancakes

Ingredients

1 tablespoon white sugar
2 teaspoons fast-acting yeast
50ml water, lukewarm
70g strong bread flour
60g plain flour
15g cornflour
¼ teaspoon salt
50ml milk, lukewarm
½ tablespoon vegetable or
groundnut oil
Plain flour for dusting

For the filling

35g unrefined dark
muscovado sugar
½ teaspoon ground cinnamon
1 pinch salt
1½ tablespoons toasted peanuts
or walnuts, finely chopped
3-4 tablespoons vegetable or
groundnut oil for frying

Equipment

Large frying pan with a lid
Rolling pin

My three-year-old daughter loves watching me cook these pancakes. It's great fun, because the dough puffs up like a balloon in the pan, and then you flatten it with a fish slice. When they're ready and you cut into them, the dark sugar filling oozes out tantalisingly. But you'll need to be patient for a few minutes – it can be very hot!

1. In a small bowl, mix the sugar, yeast and water, and leave for 5 minutes in a warm place, to activate the yeast.

2. Put the the strong bread flour, plain flour, cornflour and salt in a large bowl and make a well in the centre.

3. When the yeast mixture becomes frothy, pour it into the well and add the lukewarm milk. Mix well with your hands or chopsticks and make the dough into a ball. This will be quite soft and sticky. Place the dough in a bowl and cover with cling film. Leave in a warm place for 10 minutes.

4. Meanwhile, make the filling by mixing the dark muscovado sugar, cinnamon, salt and chopped nuts.

5. Dust a worktop with plain flour and divide the dough into 4. Using a rolling pin, roll out the dough to make 4 flat discs, about 12cm in diameter.

6. Take a quarter of the filling mix and put it in the centre of one of the discs. Lift up the sides to wrap the filling, and pinch the ends with your fingers to make sure it's sealed securely. Repeat with the other three.

7. Pour 3-4 tablespoons of oil into a large frying pan, over a medium heat.

8. You can cook all 4 pancakes at once, or do them one by one, depending on the size of your pan. When the oil is hot, put the dough parcels in the pan and cook for 30 seconds. Then turn them over and reduce the heat to medium to low and flatten out the dough with a fish slice (it should be about 1.5cm thick). Cook for another minute, then turn the pancakes over again, put a lid on, and cook for about 40-50 seconds longer. When they're cooked, put them on a cooling rack for a few minutes. They're best eaten hot – but you can reheat them in a pan if you need to.

MALAYSIAN

Chinese and Indian influences come together wonderfully in Malaysian cooking. Add a touch of Indonesian and Thai – and a few ideas from Europe – and you have a truly diverse range of aromatic, spicy flavours. The creamy sweetness of coconut milk is often used, and tropical fruits also feature prominently, as you'll see when you explore these tasty (and very easy) recipes.

Laksa Lemak

Prawn and Coconut Soup with Egg Noodles

Ingredients

12 fresh raw prawns, with their shells and heads on
2 tablespoons of groundnut oil
1 litre chicken or vegetable stock
2 lime leaves, roughly torn (optional)
800ml coconut milk
4 nests dried egg noodles
2 tablespoons fish sauce
Salt to season
150g cod or haddock fillet, cut into large chunks

For the laksa paste

1½ tablespoons coriander seeds
½ tablespoon turmeric
2 tablespoons light brown sugar
4 garlic cloves, peeled
1 lemongrass stick, roughly chopped
15g galangal, roughly chopped
A large pinch of salt
75g onion, roughly chopped
1 teaspoon shrimp paste
½ teaspoon hot chilli powder

To serve

80g beansprouts
Sliced spring onions
2 eggs, boiled and halved (optional)
40g deep fried tofu (tofu puffs), cut into small cubes
Sambal Oelek chilli sauce (optional)

Equipment

Blender

With a hint of curry and lemongrass, this prawn and coconut noodle soup is refreshing as well as satisfying. Ask your fishmonger for prawns with their shells and heads on – these make the tastiest stock.

1. Put all the laksa paste ingredients in a blender and blend until they become very smooth.

2. Take the shells and heads off the prawns.

3. Place two large pans over a medium heat and pour 1 tablespoon of oil into each one.

4. In one of the pans, fry the prawn shells and heads until they turn completely red. Pour in the chicken stock and add the lime leaves (if you're using them). Bring to the boil and simmer for 5-10 minutes.

5. In the other pan, add the laksa paste and fry it for a few minutes until the aromas start to release. Pour in the coconut milk, bring to the boil and simmer for 5-10 minutes.

6. If you're going to serve the soup with the boiled eggs, start cooking them at this stage.

7. Start cooking your noodles (follow the instructions on the pack for cooking times). You'll need to drain them and keep them warm when they're ready.

8. Using a sieve, pour the prawn stock from the first pan over the coconut broth in the second. Throw away the shells and heads.

9. Add the fish sauce to the soup and season to taste. Poach the prawns, fish and tofu puffs (if you're using them), in the soup for 3 minutes.

10. Prepare individual bowls and place the warm noodles at the bottom. Pour over the soup, sharing out the prawns and fish. Top with the beansprouts, spring onions and the boiled eggs. If you want to 'eat like a local', you can also add some Sambal Oelek sauce.

Chicken Satay with Peanut Sauce

Serves 4
15 mins preparation
10 mins cooking

Ingredients

90g shallots, peeled and finely chopped
1½ lemongrass sticks, finely chopped
3 garlic cloves, peeled and finely chopped
3 large slices of ginger, finely chopped
2 tablespoons light brown sugar
1 teaspoon chilli powder
2 teaspoons mild curry powder
2 teaspoons ketjap manis (available from oriental grocery shops and some supermarkets)
½ teaspoon salt
3 tablespoons vegetable oil
400g chicken breasts or thighs, cut into thin strips
1 bird's eye chilli, deseeded and roughly chopped
5g galangal, roughly chopped
3 teaspoons tamarind paste
60g peanut butter
1 tablespoon lime juice
30ml water
A large pinch of salt

To serve

1 small handful toasted unsalted peanuts, roughly chopped
Sliced cucumber, red onion, and lime wedges (optional)

Equipment

10-12 bamboo skewers, soaked in water
Food processor

Traditionally, these spicy, aromatic chicken skewers are grilled over charcoal, and eaten as street food – but they're just as nice cooked under the grill at home. What makes them special is the peanut dipping sauce. There are so many recipes for it, but this one bursts with flavour. Totally irresistible.

1. In a bowl, make a marinade by combining two thirds of the following ingredients: shallots, lemongrass, garlic and ginger. Then add 1 tablespoon sugar, ½ teaspoon chilli powder, all the mild curry powder and ketjap manis, ½ teaspoon of salt and 1 tablespoon of oil. Add the chicken pieces and mix well. Place cling film over the top and leave to marinade for 10 minutes.

2. Pre-heat the grill on a high setting.

3. Next, make the dipping sauce by placing the remaining shallots, lemongrass, garlic, ginger, sugar, chilli powder and oil in a food processor. Also add the bird's eye chilli and galangal, then whizz until they form a slightly coarse mixture. Add the tamarind paste, peanut butter, lime juice and water and whizz again. Taste and season with salt if necessary. If you think the sauce is too thick, you could add some more water or lime juice. Put the sauce in a bowl, ready to serve.

4. Take the skewers from the water and thread the chicken pieces onto them. Arrange them on a baking tray lined with kitchen foil and cook until they're golden brown and lightly charred on the edges – about 5-8 minutes. Turn them a few times to make sure they cook evenly.

5. Place the skewers on a large serving plate or individual plates and sprinkle with toasted peanuts. Garnish with sliced cucumber, red onion and lime wedges. Dip the chicken in the sauce and eat while it's hot or warm.

Chef's note... If you have longer than half an hour you can marinate the chicken for longer for an even deeper flavour.

Curry Puffs

Ingredients

1 teaspoon salt
175g potatoes, washed and peeled, cut into 1cm cubes
1 tablespoon vegetable oil
1 teaspoon brown or yellow mustard seeds
1 small onion, finely chopped
1 garlic clove, peeled and finely chopped
½ teaspoon white sugar
1 tablespoon mild curry powder
A few pinches of cayenne pepper (optional, if you like extra heat)
4 small curry leaves, torn in half
150ml vegetable stock
½ teaspoon tomato purée
½ teaspoon tamarind paste
1 litre vegetable oil for deep frying
Flour for dusting
180g ready-made puff pastry
90g ready-made shortcrust pastry
Mango chutney to serve

Equipment
Deep fryer
Rolling pin

In Malaysia, people from various backgrounds (Indian, Chinese and Malaysian) live together, sharing different cultures and foods. This creates new inspired dishes – such as these curry puffs, which are like a cross between a samosa and an empanada. They're a brilliant snack for curry lovers and go down very well at parties and picnics. Increase the quantities for as many people as you like!

1. Add the salt to a pan of hot water. Bring to the boil, add the potatoes and cook for 5 minutes. Drain and keep to one side.

2. In a frying pan, heat the oil and mustard seeds. When the seeds start to pop, add the onion, garlic and sugar. Fry over a medium heat for 5-7 minutes, or until the onion is golden brown.

3. Add the potatoes, curry powder, cayenne (if you're using it) and the curry leaves. Fry for a few more minutes. Pour in the vegetable stock, add the tomato purée and tamarind paste, and keep stirring until the potatoes are cooked and the curry looks slightly dry. Take off the heat and keep to one side – this is your filling.

4. Pour the oil for frying into the deep fryer and heat to 170°C.

5. Dust a worktop with flour. Using a rolling pin, roll out the puff pastry until it measures about 12cm x 20cm.

6. Also on a floured worktop, roll out the shortcrust pastry to about 12cm x 9cm. Dab it with a small amount of water, and then place it on top of the puff pastry, to one side. Fold the other side of the puff pastry over, sandwiching the shortcrust in between two layers.

7. Turn the pastry round by 90° and stretch it out until it's roughly the same rectangle shape you started with (12cm x 20cm). Don't worry if it's a bit bigger.

8. Roll the pastry into a small log. With the seam side facing down, cut it into 4 equal slices.

9. Using a rolling pin again, flatten these spirals of dough until they're about 10cm in diameter.

10. Divide the filling between the four rounds of pastry. Dab a little water around the edges, and fold them in half. Push the edges together with your fingers, and then press down on them with a fork to make sure they're properly sealed.

11. Place the curry puffs carefully in the oil. Cook them for 8 minutes, or until they're golden. Remove them from the oil, and leave to cool for a few minutes before serving with mango chutney. I love to have these with a chilled beer.

Nasi Goreng

Fried Rice

Ingredients

2 teaspoons shrimp paste
4 teaspoons sugar
4 tablespoons ketjap manis
(available from oriental grocery
shops and some supermarkets)
1 tablespoon tamarind paste
120g raw tiger prawns, shelled
and roughly chopped
240g chicken thighs,
cut into 1cm cubes
2 tablespoons groundnut oil
120g shallots,
peeled and chopped
4 garlic cloves,
peeled and finely chopped
2 red chillies, finely chopped
1 red pepper, cut into 1cm cubes
600g cooked rice
A few generous pinches of salt
A large pinch of white pepper

To serve

2 spring onions, sliced
Fried eggs
Sliced cucumber
Prawn crackers (optional)

Equipment

Large wok

This fried rice dish has a unique sweet-and-sour taste, which you get from ketjap manis (sweet soy sauce) combined with tamarind paste. You can eat Nasi Goreng as a complete meal (I've suggested some accompaniments) or you can serve it as a side, with dishes like Chicken Satay (see page 94) or Mango Chicken (see page 100).

1. In a small bowl, mix the shrimp paste, sugar, ketjap manis and tamarind paste to make a marinade. Add the prawns and chicken, stir gently to coat them and leave for 5 minutes.

2. Heat the oil in a large wok, over a high heat. Add the shallots, garlic and chillies, and fry for a few minutes before adding the red pepper. Cook for a few more minutes, then add the prawns and chicken.

3. Carry on frying until the prawns and chicken have changed colour, then add the rice. Cook for another 3-5 minutes, until everything is piping hot.

4. Season with salt and pepper and serve on individual plates or in bowls. Sprinkle with sliced spring onion, and add any of the optional garnishes suggested with the ingredients.

Chef's note... For vegetarians, simply leave out the chicken and prawns. There are still plenty of other satisfying tastes and textures in this dish.

Different brands of taramind paste vary in sourness. Some are much more acidic than others so use small amounts to start with then add more if you would prefer.

Mango Chicken

Serves 4
15 mins preparation
15 mins cooking

Ingredients

For the marinade
¼ teaspoon ground coriander
1 teaspoon grated ginger
1 teaspoon grated garlic
1½ tablespoons cornflour
4 teaspoons soy sauce
1 teaspoon white sugar

400g boneless chicken thighs,
cut into 1-inch chunks

For the sauce
3 tablespoons tomato ketchup
60ml chicken or vegetable stock
2 teaspoons white sugar
2 teaspoons soy sauce

For the rest of the recipe
¼ teaspoon cumin seeds, lightly
toasted and crushed
2 tablespoons lime juice
1 tablespoon white sugar
300g fresh mango (without the
stone), peeled and cut into chunks
1 large carrot,
peeled and sliced diagonally
1 large onion, cut into 1-inch cubes
1 red pepper, cut into 1-inch squares
2 tablespoons vegetable oil
1 red chilli, deseeded and sliced
(optional)
1 small handful cashew nuts
A few spring onions
to garnish

Equipment
Wok

This American influenced Malaysian dish is similar to Chinese sweet and sour, but uses mango chunks instead of pineapple. It's really easy to make your own sweet and sour sauce from scratch – and it's nice to try this different way of cooking chicken.

1. In a large bowl, mix all the marinade ingredients apart from the chicken.

2. Make sure there are no lumps of cornflour, and then add the chicken. Cover with cling film and marinade for 10 minutes.

3. In a small bowl, mix all the ingredients for the additional sauce.

4. Put the cumin, lime juice and sugar in a bowl and add the mango chunks. Mix thoroughly.

5. Bring a large pan of hot water to the boil, add the carrot and cook for 1 minute, then add the onion and red pepper. Cook for another minute and drain in a colander.

6. Place a wok over a high heat and add the oil. Fry the cashew nuts for a few minutes until golden, then take them out of the oil and drain on kitchen paper.

7. If you're using the red chilli, fry it in the same oil for 30 seconds, then add the chicken. Cook for 3-4 minutes over a high heat, until it turns brown. Add the carrot, onion and red pepper and cook for another 3 minutes, or until the onion has become lightly brown.

8. Add the sauce and mango. Fry for a few more minutes, until the sauce thickens slightly.

9. Top with the cashew nuts and spring onions and serve with plain boiled rice.

Nonya Pineapple Tart

Serves 4
10 mins preparation
20 mins cooking

Pineapple Jam Tart with a Hint of Cinnamon and Star Anise

Ingredients

400g fresh pineapple
(skinned and cored weight)
10g butter
50g white sugar
1 star anise
½ cinnamon stick
1 roll of ready-made sweet or
Shortcrust pastry
1 egg, lightly beaten with
1 tablespoon water

Equipment

Food processor or blender
Fine sieve
2 baking trays (1 large)
Baking parchment
Pastry brush
5cm and 3cm round cookie cutters

Malacca is my favourite town in Malaysia and this little tart is a famous local delicacy. Fresh pineapple jam, fragrant with hints of cinnamon and star anise, contrasts with the rich pastry, giving you a perfectly balanced sweet treat. In Malacca, they drink lime and plum iced tea with it, but it's great with an ordinary cuppa, too.

1. Chop the pineapple roughly and put the pieces in a food processor or blender to make a purée. Put this through a fine sieve, using a spatula to separate the pulp from the juice.

2. Melt the butter in a frying pan and fry the pineapple pulp to make a thick paste, stirring frequently.

3. Pour the pineapple juice into a small pan and add the sugar, star anise and cinnamon stick. Heat on medium to low, until the volume reduces by about three quarters. When it's very condensed, remove the star anise and cinnamon and add the pan-fried pulp to make a thick jam.

4. Spread the jam on a metal baking tray to cool down.

5. Pre-heat the oven to 190°C/fan 170°C/gas mark 5. Roll out the pastry, and cut out 24 round discs, 5cm in diameter. Put 12 of them on a large baking tray lined with baking parchment and brush with egg wash.

6. Use a 3cm round cutter to cut the centres out of the remaining 12 discs. Place each of the circles you've made on the top of the first 12 pastry discs, and push the edges with a fork to make patterns like sun rays.

7. Fill a bowl with water. Use this to keep wetting your hands as you divide the pineapple filling into 12 balls. Place each ball in the centre of a pastry, and flatten it slightly. (If you have time, make thin strips from the leftover pastry and use these to create criss-cross patterns on top, and brush with egg wash.)

8. Put the tarts in the oven and cook for 15-20 minutes, until they're lightly browned. Let them cool down slightly before serving.

Tropical Fruit Salad with Passion Fruit Syrup

Ingredients

900g of your choice of tropical
fruits, such as:
Melon, mangoes, dragon fruit,
papaya, strawberries, mangosteens,
passion fruit, longan, star fruit,
watermelon, lychees
1 tablespoon water

For the passion fruit syrup
80ml water
100g white sugar
A few very thin slices of lemon,
pith removed
Grated zest from the rest of
the lemon
2 tablespoons lemon juice
2 tablespoons fresh passion fruit
juice (from about 2 fruits)

Lemon zest to garnish

When you're dealing with the wonderful flavours of tropical fruit, it's best to keep things simple. Here we just slice the fruit and pour over a freshly made passion fruit syrup. The perfect end to a meal – or even a special breakfast.

1. Heat the water and sugar in a small saucepan, over a high heat. When it's boiling add the lemon slices and zest, then turn down the heat and simmer for 10 minutes.

2. Add the lemon juice and passion fruit juice and dunk the base of the pan in a bowl of cold water to cool the syrup down.

3. Meanwhile, slice the fruits and place them in a large bowl. Pour half the syrup over and toss lightly.

4. Divide the fruits between four bowls, and pour the remaining syrup over the top. Garnish with lemon zest, and serve with iced tea.

Rice

A staple part of Asian cooking. By simply adding different ingredients to plain rice, you can create a tasty side dish in minutes.

Serves 4

Ingredients
320g uncooked jasmine or short grain rice
(makes 700g cooked rice)
440ml cold water

Plain Boiled Rice

1. Wash and drain the rice. Put it in a medium-sized pan and add 440ml of cold water. Place the lid on and bring to the boil. When the lid starts to rattle, turn the heat down to its lowest setting and cook for 12 minutes. Take the pan off the heat and, keeping the lid on, leave the rice to steam for another 10 minutes.

Serves 4-6

Ingredients
4g dried wakame seaweed, soaked in warm water
½ teaspoon soy sauce
a pinch of salt and white sugar
600g hot cooked rice
(about 4 bowls of rice)
2 teaspoon toasted sesame seeds

Wakame, White Sesame and Soy Rice

1. Once the wakame is soft, squeeze out the water with your hands and chop the wakame into small pieces, about 5-6mm flakes. Put them in a bowl and add the soy sauce, salt and sugar. Mix well and leave for 10 minutes.

2. Having done that add the wakame mix into the cooked rice and mix well. Sprinkle sesame seeds on the top and serve immediately.

From left to right: Gomashio, Plain Boiled Rice, Carrots, Egg and Sesame Fried Rice, Wakame, White Sesame and Soy Rice

Carrots, Egg and Sesame Fried Rice

Serves 4

Ingredients
1 tablespoon of vegetable oil
2 eggs, lightly beaten
2 small carrots, peeled and
cut into small pieces
1 garlic clove, peeled
and finely chopped
600g hot cooked rice
(about 4 bowls of rice)
1 teaspoon sesame oil
1 teaspoon sesame seeds
Few large pinches of salt and
generous amount of white pepper

1. Heat a frying pan on a medium to high heat and pour in half a tablespoon of oil. Cook the eggs and lightly mix on the pan until they have set. Transfer the cooked eggs on a plate and set aside.

2. Pour the remaining oil to the pan and cook the carrots and garlic for few minutes. Lightly season and add the rice. Stir well and once the carrots and rice are mixed, add the eggs back in the pan and pour sesame oil. Stir again and add the sesame seeds. Season to taste and serve immediately.

Gomashio (black sesame and salt seasoning)

Serves 4-6

Ingredients
1 teaspoon sea salt
2 tablespoons black or white
sesame seeds

1. Grind the salt slightly using a pestle and mortar, then add the sesame seeds and grind more until you have a coarse mixture. Sprinkle over plain boiled rice. Sesame salt can be kept in an airtight container for up to a week.

Dipping Sauces

A dipping sauce works as a delicious accompaniment to many different Asian dishes.

Soy, Apple and Ginger Sauce (for grilled meat)

Ingredients
½ tablespoon rice wine vinegar
50ml soy sauce
1 tablespoon mirin
½ green apple
40g onion
½ garlic clove
2 teaspoons honey

1. Put all the ingredients in a blender and blend until smooth. Serve with grilled meat. This will keep in a fridge for up to a week.

Wasabi Mayonnaise

Ingredients
4 tablespoons mayonnaise
1½ teaspoon wasabi paste
½ teaspoon soy sauce
2 teaspoons water to loosen

1. Combine the wasabi paste, soy sauce and water in a small bowl, stir well to form a paste and add the mayonnaise. Store, covered with cling film, in the refrigerator until ready to serve.

2. Serve with grilled or fried fish, steak or French fries.

From left to right: Soy, Apple and Ginger Sauce, Wasabi Mayonnaise, Sushi Vinegar, Nouc Cham Sweet Chilli Sauce, Sesame Sauce, Spicy Sriracha Chilli Sauce

Sushi Vinegar

Ingredients

4 tablespoons rice wine vinegar
2 tablespoons sugar
½ teaspoon salt
Dash of soy sauce

1. Put all the ingredients in a small pan and warm up until the sugar dissolves. Leave to cool and mix the vinegar in piping hot cooked rice to make sushi rolls or edamame rice (see page 38).

Nouc Cham Sweet Chilli Sauce

Ingredients

30g white sugar,
diluted with 45ml cold water
3 tablespoons lime juice
2 tablespoons fish sauce
2 garlic cloves,
peeled and finely chopped
2 red chillies,
deseeded and finely chopped
Salt to season

1. Combine all the ingredients apart from the garlic and red chilli.

2. Once the sugar has dissolved completely add the garlic and chilli.

3. Season with salt to taste.

Sesame Sauce

Ingredients

5 tablespoons tahini
(sesame seed paste)
2 tablespoons white sugar
5 tablespoons soy sauce
1 teaspoon grated ginger
3 tablespoons rice wine vinegar

1. Mix all the ingredients in a small bowl and serve with grilled pork steak, or drizzle over sliced roast pork belly.

About Howdens Joinery

Howdens Joinery offers a range of integrated kitchens, appliances and joinery products designed to meet the needs of modern living.

Our offer includes over 50 different kitchen designs, plus a full range of accessories, worktops, doors, flooring, skirting, and a wide variety of Lamona appliances, sinks and taps, exclusive to Howdens. The Lamona range has been selected to perfectly complement our range of kitchens and products are manufactured to the highest standards to ensure they are durable and reliable. Last year we supplied over 365,000 kitchens, 650,000 appliances and 550,000 sinks and taps to UK homes.

Sleek and simple, with features such as natural finishes, dark colours to set the tone and some paler neutral highlights - these are the hallmarks of a classic Asian kitchen. Plus, of course, all the practical accessories and clever storage that make those delicious dishes easy to prepare.

To find out more or locate one of over 610 nationwide depots, visit **www.howdens.com**

Lamona Professional 5 Burner Gas Hob

Bespoke Breakfast Bar Seating Area

Lamona Single Fan Ovens with Lamona Warming Drawers

Lamona Belmont Single Bowl Sink with Lamona Chrome Roya Swan Neck Monobloc Tap

Bespoke Seating Area

About the author

Cookery writer and creative food stylist Seiko Hatfield grew up just outside Tokyo, where her passion for cooking began. Each day after school, she would stop at her grandparents' farm to pick up fresh vegetables, and then run home to help her mother prepare the evening meal.

Seiko studied at Tokyo Kasei University of Home Economics, and developed her culinary knowledge on extensive travels around South East Asia and the Far East, absorbing an exciting and exotic range of influences.

Arriving in the UK 15 years ago, she began to work as head chef for a Yorkshire Life Restaurant of the Year, creating inventive dishes that made the very best of fresh, local produce – just as she had done as a child. It wasn't long before she set up a successful private dining and food business of her own, called 'SushiGirl'.

These days, Seiko spends much of her time in London, where she has worked for a number of years as the principal recipe writer and stylist for Harrods Magazine. She also contributes to TV and press advertising campaigns, and her work often appears in publications such as The Sunday Times, Vogue and Fabulous.

Although Seiko is Japanese, she is experienced in all Asian cooking. Writing the recipes for this book has given her a wonderful opportunity to return to her roots and remember her earlier exploration of this diverse continent.

Exclusive to Howdens Joinery Co.

www.lamona.co.uk